How Firm A Foundation
William Bradford and Plymouth

John M. Pafford

Heritage Books, Inc.

Published 2002 by

HERITAGE BOOKS, INC.
1540E Pointer Ridge Place
Bowie, Maryland 20716

1-800-398-7709
www.heritagebooks.com

ISBN 0-7884-2140-9

A Complete Catalog Listing Hundreds of Titles
On History, Genealogy, and Americana
Available Free Upon Request

To Martha,

with love and appreciation.

CONTENTS

PREFACE

Well-known yet not much studied today, the Pilgrims have been covered with an almost mystical aura, resulting in too little serious consideration of their impressive achievements and a failure to see them as real human beings rather than semi-legendary figures. They deserve more.

I grew up in Falmouth on Cape Cod, not far from where the Pilgrims first landed and within a few miles of where they settled at Plymouth. Sadly, though, this very nearness led to my not finding William Bradford and Plymouth as interesting as further away people and places until I reached my middle years. Then I came to realize that I had given short shrift to a great man and to an interesting group of people who accomplished much.

The Pilgrims laid the foundation for the future United States--Christian faith, recognition that a good society must have virtue, order, and freedom balancing community and individualism. They also demonstrated entrepreneurship, the work ethic, and saw clearly the need for effective armed forces. They gave us too Thanksgiving, one of the most revered American holidays. Although Jamestown earlier had set aside a time for thanksgiving, it is to the Pilgrims that we still look each year when the day appears again.

The American romance with this group of vibrant, adventurous, mostly young people has not faded. Plymouth today is a busy tourist center visited annually by about 500,000 persons. Families and individuals come to see the Plymouth Rock, to ponder the small size of the replica Mayflower II, to walk through Plimouth Plantation, the reconstructed 1627 village, and to buy souvenirs. The harbor, which never really developed as a commercial port, is used mostly by pleasure boats.

A sense of awe and respect still characterizes the public attitude toward the Pilgrims. Will it last? Surely as long as there is anyone moved by the principles which drove these remarkable people. Samuel Eliot Morison perhaps said it best:

> The place of the Pilgrim Fathers in American history can best be stated by a paradox. Of slight importance in their own time, they are of great and increasing significance in our time, through the influence of their story on American folklore and tradition. And the key to that story, the vital factor in this little group, is the faith in God that exalted them and their small enterprise to something of lasting value and enduring interest.[1]

Gary North considered the reputation of Plymouth to be overblown. He talked of their being better known than their Puritan neighbors to the north. Yet, he said, Massachusetts Bay was more significant. "It was Gov. John Winthrop, not Gov. William Bradford who left his mark on American institutions."[2]

Certainly there is much to admire in John Winthrop and Massachusetts Bay, but more precedents were set, more examples given by Plymouth. There the Christian commonwealth was somewhat milder. There government responsible to the people developed first. There the principle

---

[1] Samuel Eliot Morison, "The Pilgrim Fathers in History," *By Land and By Sea* (New York: Alfred A. Knopf, 1953), p. 234.

[2] Gary North, *Puritan Economic Experiments* (Tyler, Texas: Institute for Christian Economics, 1988), p. 22.

that able-bodied men trained militarily and were prepared to fight for their freedom developed first. There a market-oriented economy developed first. They authored the Mayflower Compact, singled out by Daniel Boorstin as "the primary document of self-government in the British colonies in North America."[3]

William Bradford was the dominant person in Plymouth until his death in 1657. Although governing a colony which never became rich or powerful, his prestige as a man of Christian integrity, wisdom, courage, and ability extended beyond its borders, surmounting the small scale of the venue within which he labored. Far from being merely the governor and chronicler of a small colony in seventeenth century New England, Bradford is considered the first great American political figure and the first American historian of significance. Samuel Eliot Morison, in the preface to his edition of Bradford's *Of Plymouth Plantation*, wrote of the book and its author:

> Many English and American historians and literary critics have praised it as one of the greatest books of the seventeenth century, and have declared that the Governor's name should rank little lower than those of Milton, Bunyan and of King James's translators of the Bible.[4]

---

[3] Daniel J. Boorstin, *Hidden History* (New York: Harper and Row, 1987), p. 67.

[4] William Bradford, *Of Plymouth Plantation*, Samuel Eliot Morison, ed. (New York: Alfred A. Knopf, 1996), p. vii.

In the following pages, he will be considered in conjunction with Plymouth during his almost forty years of service there.

BEGINNINGS

Born in Austerfield, Yorkshire in 1590, William Bradford
was the third child and only son of solid, middle class
parents.[*] His father, after whom he was named, was a
yeoman[**] and his mother, Alice, a daughter of a shopkeeper.
Orphaned by the age of eight, he was raised by relatives.
Losing both parents at an early age, then a grandfather with
whom he then lived, could have made young William bitter
and rebellious. Instead, it strengthened him without making
him impervious to the feelings and needs of others. As a
youth, his health was poor, giving him the opportunity to
supplement his sketchy formal schooling with private
reading, an interest which remained with him through the
rest of his life. He outgrew whatever it was which had
afflicted him and became a robust man.

At the age of twelve, Bradford turned seriously to the
study of the Bible and subsequently joined a group of
Puritans who met at the home of William Brewster in the
nearby village of Scrooby, a group which in 1606 separated
totally from the Church of England and organized itself as an
independent parish. Brewster, a member of the gentry class
who had spent some time studying at Cambridge[***] and then

---

[*] Most of what is known of Bradford's early years came from Cotton
Mather, the seventeenth century Massachusetts Bay churchman and
scholar who apparently drew upon now lost material written by Bradford.
No portrait nor physical description of him exists. The only known portrait
of one of the Pilgrims is that of Edward Winslow.

[**] Yeomen were freeholders below the gentry who farmed their own lands.

[***] At this time, most of the graduates of Oxford and Cambridge were
young men headed for the clergy. There were, though, attending those
universities sons of good families taking what Morison referred to as "a
relatively easy course in ancient literature and history that led to no
degree." (Samuel Eliot Morison, *The Intellectual Life of Colonial New England*

served as private secretary to William Davison, a prominent Elizabethan diplomat, was the bailiff (overseer) at the manor house which was owned by the Archbishop of York. He saw promise in young Bradford and guided his reading. Bradford would become an impressive, self-taught scholar whose library and writings would reflect his reading of Calvin, Zwingli, Beza, Peter Martyr, Luther, Erasmus, Ovid, Pliny, Seneca, Marcus Aurelius, Plato, Bodin, and Guicciardini. At his death, he left a library of almost three hundred books-- impressive for that time.[5] Bradford probably learned Latin from Brewster. Later in life, he taught himself Greek and Hebrew.[6]

Across England at this time those labeled Puritans wished to rid the Church of England of the episcopal form of government and liturgical worship, both of which they rejected as carry-overs from Roman Catholicism. Some worked within the Church to effect the desired changes, others, such as the Scrooby congregation, separated entirely. During the closing years of the reign of Elizabeth (1558-1603), Puritan opposition smoldered, but was held in check by a modest degree of toleration and by the veneration accorded her by most of her subjects who recognized all that she had done to ensure the security of England, especially from Spain, and to increase the prosperity and power of the country. To a degree, Elizabeth had been willing to leave alone dissenters

---

[New York: New York University Press, 1965], pp. 20-21). Apparently Brewster fell in this category.

[5] Samuel Eliot Morison, *The Intellectual Life of Colonial New England* (New York: New York University Press, 1965), pp. 134-135; Bradford Smith, *Bradford of Plymouth* (Philadelphia: J. B. Lippincott Company, 1951), p. 305.

[6] Perry D. Westbrook, *William Bradford* (Boston: Twayne Publishers, 1978), pp. 97, 102-103.

from the Church of England as long as they were discreet and posed no political threat. Her successor, James I (1603-1625), however, was determined to enforce religious conformity. Because of this growing restrictiveness, many of the Puritans chose voluntary exile in the Netherlands where they could worship in freedom.

In 1607, the Scrooby congregation joined this exodus, settling down in Leyden under the leadership of their minister, John Robinson. Here Bradford, drawing upon the modest bequest from his dead parents which became his at twenty-one, went into business as a fustian (linen and cotton) maker. Business, however, did not prosper. Here too he married and became the father of a son.

For many of these exiles, though, there would develop an alternative preferable to the Netherlands.

The English permitted religious dissidents such as these people, but also including Roman Catholics and Quakers, to emigrate to the New World where they could establish colonies, worship freely, and remain loyal subjects of the crown. This benefited both parties. The dissidents enjoyed more freedom than they had at home and the English government gained an expanding colonial population, a significant economic and military consideration, while reducing dissent in Great Britain. This logical and advantageous course of action was rejected by the French who permitted only faithful Roman Catholics to settle in North America. The English had a superior navy and the English colonies had a more moderate climate and more arable land, but French restrictiveness was the major drag on their growth in the New World. There was no way for the Huguenots (French Protestants) to be true both to their Church and to their country. This policy was to cost the

French dearly in their rivalry with the British for domination of North America. New France (Canada) never developed a population base to match that of the British colonies to its south.

Francis Parkman recognized the deadening effect of French centralized absolutism as compared with the often imperfect, sometimes inconsistent English commitment to freedom. As he wrote of New England:

...yet the vital juices of the root penetrated at last to the uttermost branches, and nourished them to an irrepressible strength and expansion. With New France it was otherwise. She was consistent to the last. Root, stem, and branch, she was the nursling of authority.... Her records shine with glorious deeds, the self-devotion of heroes and of martyrs; and the result of all is disorder, imbecility, ruin.[7]

[7] Francis Parkman, *France and England in North America*, Vol. I: *Pioneers of France in the New World* (New York: Literary Classics of the United States, Inc., 1983), p. 312.

TO THE NEW WORLD

In 1617, the English exiles in Leyden determined to leave the Netherlands. They were concerned lest their children, speaking Dutch and attending Dutch schools, cease to be English. Also, the possibility of war between the Netherlands and Spain loomed before them with the possibility that Spain would win and destroy religious freedom. Of particular significance to them was the prospect of establishing their own Christian community as English citizens in the New World. They sought support for their project in England.*

Many monied Englishmen were attracted by the possibility for profit through investing in settlements in North America. The Virginia Company had been granted jurisdiction by King James over the area extending from 34° to 41° north latitude, from what today is southern North Carolina up to New York City and Long Island.

Thomas Weston headed a group of London merchants** who offered to bankroll these prospective settlers. They

---

* Albert J. Nock, a mid-twentieth century libertarian thinker, held the off-beat belief that many of the institutions established by the Pilgrims in Plymouth were not English in origin, but rather reflected their experiences in the Netherlands. Here, he alleged, they derived their educational concepts, belief in local self-government, and much of their criminal and civil codes. Albert J. Nock, *Our Enemy, The State* (Tampa, Florida: Hallberg Publishing Corporation, 1996), pp. 63-64.

Although these institutions did develop in the Netherlands, it is not accurate to view the Pilgrims as other than solidly English. They were Christians before all else, but definitely Christians who were clearly English.

** They are often referred to as "adventurers," not because of their seeking thrills, but because of their venturing their money. Bradford used the word to distinguish those who financially backed the enterprise from the "colonists" or "planters," those who crossed the Atlantic to establish the new settlement.

demanded of them that there be no private ownership of land or houses. After seven years, everything would be divided equally between the investors and the colonists. The settlers were refused the two days a week they sought to work for themselves and were required to devote all their efforts to the common cause. This was opposed by leaders such as Bradford, but the harsh terms which had been accepted by their representative, Robert Cushman, were agreed to because of the fear that the choices were this agreement or nothing.

By insisting upon these stipulations, the merchants were not demonstrating communistic or socialistic views, but rather their belief that they would recoup their investments quicker and profit more. As would be seen in a few years, they were wrong in their assumption because they did not understand human nature, specifically what stimulated the incentive to produce.

The settlers have come to be known historically as the Pilgrims. Bradford used that word in his history:

> So they left that goodly and pleasant city which had been their resting place near twelve years [Leyden]; but they knew they were pilgrims,[*] and looked not much on those things, but lift up their eyes to the heavens, their dearest country, and quieted their spirits.[8]

They secured the services of two ships, the Mayflower and the Speedwell. The latter, though, leaked badly, aborting

---

[*] Here Bradford referred the reader to Hebrews 11:13-16.

[8] Bradford, *Of Plymouth Plantation*, p. 47.

two attempts in August to leave for the New World. Finally, they gave up on the Speedwell as unseaworthy and decided to go with just the Mayflower. She was commanded by Captain Christopher Jones, an experienced fifty-year-old seaman and the son of a sea captain. He owned a one-fourth interest in the vessel.

On September 6, 1620[*], the Mayflower sailed from Plymouth, England with her 102 passengers and about thirty crewmen. The ship, 180 tons and probably approximately 100 feet long (her exact dimensions are not known), was then about twelve years old and had spent most of her career engaged in carrying wine from France. As was recorded intriguingly by Samuel Eliot Morison in a footnote to his edition of Bradford's history:

> The ullage from wine casks is known to have neutralized the filth that the sailors of that day left in the bilge and to have made a "sweet ship," which may explain why the Mayflower got all but one of her passengers across alive, despite a late season and tempestuous voyage.[9]

Be that as it may, the crowded conditions, primitive sanitary facilities, limited privacy, poor food, plus chill and damp quarters were unhealthy enough and proved the faith and determination of the Pilgrims. Still, only one passenger

---

[*] Some confusion in dates may arise because England at this time had not yet adopted the Gregorian calendar which had been introduced by Pope Gregory XIII in 1582, establishing our present calendar. England finally would do so in 1752. At the time Plymouth was settled, the old Julian calendar was ten days behind. Therefore, by the calendar of today, the Mayflower sailed on September 16.

[9] Bradford, *Of Plymouth Plantation*, p. 52n.

died during the voyage, William Butten, a servant to Samuel Fuller, the Pilgrim's physician. Since one child, Oceanus Hopkins, had been born, the number remained the same at 102.

Of the 102, forty-one were members of the Leyden congregation. Three of them (Brewster, his wife, and Bradford) had been members of the Scrooby Church. The rest of the Mayflower's passengers were referred to as "strangers."[10] They had been added to the roster of prospective colonists by the London merchants backing the venture to increase their numbers so as to make profitability more likely and to provide specific skills such as Myles Standish, the military leader, and John Alden, a cooper. It is not certain how many of them were Christian, but the colony would have some tensions because of the "mixed multitude."[11] In spite of this, the colony's spiritual and public policy foundations would be sound thanks to the influence of such men as William Bradford, William Brewster, John Carver, and Edward Winslow.

On November 9, a lookout sighted the highlands above the outer beach of Cape Cod.* Backed by forests of oak, beech, and evergreens, the dunes rose a hundred feet above the

---

[10] *Ibid.*, p. 44.

[11] Exodus 12:38; Numbers 11:4-6.

* Perhaps Phoenicians sailed along this coast a thousand years before the birth of Christ. Probably Vikings did so a thousand years after His birth. For over a century prior to the voyage of the Mayflower, European explorers, traders, and fishermen had been passing by the area, sometimes landing briefly. Bartholomew Gosnold was here in 1602, giving Cape Cod its name because of the profusion of cod. John Smith, better known for his activities in Virginia, sailed New England waters in 1614 and mapped the coast down to Cape Cod.

shore. Sixty-four days had elapsed since they had sailed west from England, a long, hard voyage even by seventeenth century standards. The ship turned south to pass around the Cape and head through Long Island Sound to an area near the mouth of the Hudson River.[12] Although the Dutch claimed this region in 1609 as a result of Hudson's voyage, the English rejected the claim and Manhattan Island remained unsettled by the Dutch until 1626.

Encountering contrary winds, shoals, and breakers off Monomoy Point, the southeastern extension of Cape Cod, the Mayflower turned back northward, rounded the northern tip of the Cape, and on November 11 anchored in the lee of what today is Provincetown. There a service of thanksgiving was held, rejoicing in the completion of a perilous journey during which most were sick and all were miserable; the combination of cold and storm had made it all but impossible to dry sodden woolen clothes. Now the passengers and crew could dry out, seek fresh water and food, and, perhaps, find a location for their permanent settlement.

They faced first, though, the necessity to regularize their governmental status. Since they had landed north of territory controlled by the Virginia Company from whom they held a patent*, they had to formulate a political compact. This they did the day after the Mayflower dropped anchor with the justly famous Mayflower Compact. It was signed by all free adult males and, probably, some, but not all, adult male servants. Bradford did not list those who signed when he wrote his history. Nathaniel Morton, Bradford's nephew,

---

[12] Bradford, *Of Plymouth Plantation*, p. 60.

* It is not known what the patent specified concerning the area to be settled.

arrived in Plymouth in 1623. Writing in 1669, he did provide what hopefully is an accurate roster.[13]

In the Name of God, Amen.

We whose names are underwritten, the loyal subjects of our dread Sovereign Lord King James, by the Grace of God of Great Britain, France, and Ireland King, Defender of the Faith, etc.

Having undertaken, for the Glory of God and advancement of the Christian Faith and Honour of our King and Country, a Voyage to plant the First Colony in the Northern Parts of Virginia, do by these presents solemnly and mutually in the presence of God and one of another, Covenant and Combine ourselves together into a Civil Body Politic, for our better ordering and preservation and furtherance of the ends aforesaid; and by virtue hereof to enact, constitute and frame such just and equal Laws, Ordinances, Acts, Constitutions and Offices, from time to time, as shall be thought most meet and convenient for the general good of the Colony, unto which we promise all due submission and obedience. In witness whereof we have hereunder subscribed our names at Cape Cod, the 11th of November, in the year of the reign of our Sovereign Lord King James, of England, France and Ireland the eighteenth, and of Scotland the fifty-fourth. Anno Domini 1620.[14]

---

[13] Nathaniel Morton, *New England's Memoriall* (Bowie, Maryland: Heritage Books, Inc., 1997), p. 26.

[14] Bradford, *Of Plymouth Plantation*, pp. 75-76.

The signatories affirmed their loyalty to the Crown and committed themselves to further British interests in the New World. Of particular significance, though, is their stating that the colony was being established "for the glory of God and advancement of the Christian Faith." Their Christianity was not something compartmentalized and limited to church activities, but rather permeated every aspect of their lives, including being the foundation of their government.

So that order and justice could exist, they pledged their obedience to a government which was authorized to make laws for the "general good of the Colony." The government was to function under God, within the British Empire, and with the consent of the governed. During the years of the Plymouth Colony (1620-1692), there would be full compatibility between these points. John Carver, a prosperous London merchant, was chosen as the first governor.

The Pilgrims' philosophy of government predated John Locke who often is credited with being the most significant thinker in terms of providing the rationale for American independence. As a political philosopher, though, his influence has been more limited with the firmly Christian. Locke very well could have been a Christian, but, if so, he separated his political theory from his faith. His position rested on natural law rather than on revelation. According to Locke, the origin of government is a social contract entered into by the people and their government with rights and obligations on each side. The people yield some of their individual freedoms in return for governmental protection of life, liberty, and property. Governments exist and derive their powers from the consent of the governed, a far cry from the Biblical teaching that governments were ordained by God. Russell Kirk wrote that "Locke has nothing to say about the Christian view of society as a bond between God and man...."[15] The Pilgrims understood that the consent of the governed is a key factor in determining the legitimacy of a government, but they placed the sovereignty of God and fidelity to His Word at the highest level.

In many respects, this group of people was the most remarkable of any who came to what would become the United States. By and large they were people of strong Christian faith who were willing to pray, to fight, and to work to build a Christian commonwealth. Most were young, only four being fifty or older and only four others were between forty and fifty. The key leaders were in their thirties, some in their twenties. What made them unusual was that the Pilgrims were mostly of the yeoman and artisan classes--landowning family farmers and skilled tradesmen. There were no members of the aristocracy, the gentry, or university educated professionals among them, William Brewster being the exception. They demonstrated the capability of the average God-fearing Englishman for orderly, just self-government.

Although the people of Plymouth did not have much in the way of formal education, there were at least a few books in most homes and some libraries were, by the standards of the time, moderately impressive. William Brewster had the largest, numbering approximately four hundred volumes. William Bradford's, discussed previously,* contained some of the most significant writings in Western Civilization, works

---

[15] Russell Kirk, *The Roots of American Order* (LaSalle, Illinois: Open Court, 1977), p. 287.

* See p. 2.

12

of theology, history, and literature. Myles Standish had copies of Caesar's *Commentaries* and of *The Swedish Intelligencer* which covered the campaigns of Gustavus Adolphus.[16]

Samuel Eliot Morison caught the essence of the Pilgrims in these few words:

> Here is a story of a simple people impelled by an ardent faith in God to a dauntless courage in danger, a boundless resourcefulness in face of difficulty, an impregnable fortitude in adversity. It strengthens and inspires us still, after more than three centuries, in this age of change and uncertainty.[17]

---

[16] Morison, *The Intellectual Life of Colonial New England*, p. 134.

[17] Morison, "The Pilgrim Fathers in History," pp. 235-236.

EXPLORATION

On November 15, a force of sixteen men commanded by Myles Standish landed to explore the land off which the Mayflower lay anchored. Among them was William Bradford. Standish, about thirty-six years of age, was a professional soldier who had fought the Spaniards in the Netherlands and would serve ably as the military leader of Plymouth. As the expedition moved inland, they spotted a small group of Indians who fled from them. The next day, the Pilgrims followed their track on to the outer Cape dunes. They lost the trail when the Indians turned back inland through dense thickets.

During their time ashore, they came upon an Indian deer trap--a sapling bent down, a rope noose attached to it concealed under leaves with acorns scattered on top. The idea was for a browsing deer to step into the area of the noose, dislodge whatever was keeping the sapling bent, whereupon the sapling would spring upright with the deer caught by the leg. Stephen Hopkins spotted it. As it was being examined, Bradford, who had been in the rear of the column, was careless, stepped into the danger zone, was caught by the leg, and there he was--upside down, no doubt subjected to the expected rough male humor before being cut down.[18]

The explorers did discover fresh water and a location where the Indians had farmed, built a dwelling,* and buried

---

[18] G. Mourt, *A Relation or Journal of the beginning and proceedings of the English Plantation settled at Plymouth in New England, by certain English adventurers both merchants and others*. Hereinafter referred to as *Mourt's Relation* (Bedford, Massachusetts: Applewood Books, 1963), p. 23.

* The typical Indian dwelling in New England at this time was a frame of saplings lashed together, overlaid with woven mats and strips of bark sewn together with evergreen tree roots. A hole in the center permitted smoke to rise and leave.

their dead. They also found buried baskets of corn, part of which they took and reburied the rest. A second landing carried away more corn and beans which the Pilgrims needed both for food over the winter and for planting in the spring. About six months later, after making contact with the Indians who lived there, the Pilgrims paid for what they had taken.

This area was unacceptable for a permanent settlement since the mouth of the Pamet River in what today is Truro, could accommodate small boats only, making it useless as a port. A further expedition, again including Bradford, took the Mayflower's shallop* and headed south in Cape Cod Bay in search of a better location. By now it was early December** and the weather had become colder, the spray freezing on the men as they sailed south, then turned east to land in what today is Eastham. That night, they built a barricade of logs, stakes, and pine boughs around their camp in case the Indians were hostile. They arose about 5:00 a.m., prayed, and prepared to sail on. Some of the men carried their firearms down to the boat, left them there, and came back to the camp for breakfast while they waited for the tide to turn. Then a loud cry rang out and they came under arrow attack. Those who had kept their weapons returned fire while the others

---

* The typical shallop was a double-ended boat with a single mast, somewhat over thirty feet long with a beam of about nine feet.

** On December 7, the day after they left, Bradford's wife, Dorothy, was drowned. He did not learn of it until the expedition returned several days later. It is not known for certain whether she fell accidentally over the side of the Mayflower during the night or whether she committed suicide, although Bradford's not commenting on the cause of death in his writings tends to give credence to the latter. Their five-year-old son, John, had been left behind in England with Dorothy's parents. Later he joined his father in Plymouth.

hurried to regain theirs. Wielding their cutlasses, some of them wearing coats of mail, they rushed to their stacked muskets and joined in the skirmish. Bradford, a participant in the fray, recorded that one of the Indians stood his ground behind a tree and exchanged fire with the Pilgrims, bow against musket, until a shot splintered the bark near his ear and discouraged him from further action. There were no Pilgrim casualties, although several coats of mail were hit. Indian losses were not mentioned, but there is no indication that they were serious.[19]

They now sailed on, heading westward across the bay. After several hours, the weather started to deteriorate; it began to rain and snow, the wind increased, and the water became rough. The rudder on the shallop broke, necessitating their steering with a couple of oars. They then sighted an inlet for which they steered. Before gaining it, the mast broke as the storm worsened. Coming in with the flood tide, though, they gained shelter, arriving safely in the place where they would settle.* After the storm cleared, they sounded the harbor, finding it deep enough for small ships, and explored inland. The expedition encountered no Indians, but their earlier presence there was evident from the cleared cornfields. Fresh water was abundant and just back from the

---

[19] G. Mourt, *Mourt's Relation*, pp. 69-70.

* Possibly they landed on Plymouth Rock, but Bradford stated nothing about it, nor do other Pilgrim records make any mention of it. The story only emerged about 150 years later when Ephraim Spooner told the tale in 1769 at the Old Colony Club in Plymouth. The account is appealing, but as an historical site, the Plymouth Rock cannot be authenticated. (George F. Willison, *The Pilgrim Reader: The Story of the Pilgrims As Told By Themselves and Their Contemporaries Friendly and Unfriendly* [Garden City, New York: Doubleday and Company, Inc., 1953], p. 566.)

harbor there was high ground for defense. The date was December 11. The expedition now returned across Cape Cod Bay to the Mayflower and reported the good news concerning the site. On December 26, the Mayflower anchored off Plymouth and the colony began.

THE NEW COLONY

During these years, as British colonization began in North America, probably only about 750,000 Indians inhabited what today is the United States. Further south, advanced Indian civilizations in Mexico, Central America, and northwestern South America had substantially larger populations.[20]

The area around Plymouth, inhabited by Patuxets, part of the Massachusetts tribe, had been decimated by smallpox a few years prior to the arrival of the Pilgrims. Fear of the disease kept other Indians from moving in. When this was combined with cleared fields waiting to be planted, an excellent natural harbor, fresh water, and militarily defensible high ground, the result was a more favorable set of circumstances than the new settlers could have found elsewhere. They saw the blessings of God on their determination to establish a Christian commonwealth in the New World.

The Wampanoags controlled what today is southeastern Massachusetts, beginning just south of Plymouth. The smallpox plague had weakened them, leaving them vulnerable to their enemies, the Narragansetts, who had not been so hit by the disease. The Wampanoags, therefore, would become interested in the Pilgrims as allies. They had learned of European wealth and power not only from their own contacts with traders and fishermen, but also from Squanto, of whom more later.

The settlers at Plymouth now faced a time of great hardship with the onset of winter. Their supplies were limited and, due to the lateness of their arrival, no crops had been grown. They set about building homes, initially along

---

[20] Carl Waldman, *Atlas of the North American Indian* (New York: Facts on File Publications, 1985), p. 29.

both sides of a single street stretching up the hill from the waterfront. A second street was laid out intersecting the main street at right angles. The first homes had one room, generally with a loft above. They probably had few, if any, windows. None has survived to the present. As more substantial homes were constructed, these earlier structures perhaps became barns or sheds. At first, buildings were mud daub and wattle, but soon plank construction became the standard. Thatched roofs were common until around 1635 when their popularity faded due to the fire hazard.[21]

As Plymouth became more settled, larger homes were built. Typically, they had two rooms with a central fireplace and two rooms in the loft. Floors were of wood. Until about 1640, windows were covered by cloth or oiled paper; thereafter glass came into general use. Often a lean-to was added to the back or side of a house as a kitchen, as additional sleeping space, or for storage.[22]

To aid as much as possible and to avoid a winter crossing of the North Atlantic, The Mayflower remained at Plymouth through the first winter. During this time, half the colonists died. Hunting and fishing helped to feed the populace, but still poor diet and the debilitating effects of the long voyage had weakened many. Bradford wrote that January and February were the worst of months for suffering, that sometimes two or three people would die each day. Yet during these months determination remained strong and Christian charity was impressive. As Bradford recorded of this time when barely fifty colonists remained:

---

[21] John Demos, *A Little Commonwealth: Family Life in Plymouth Colony* (New York: Oxford University Press, 1970), pp. 25-28.

[22] *Ibid.*, pp. 29-33.

And of these, in the time of most distress, there was but six or seven sound persons who to their great commendations, be it spoken, spared no pains night nor day, but with abundance of toil and hazard of their own health, fetched them wood, made them fires, dressed them meat, made their beds, washed their loathsome clothes, clothed and unclothed them. In a word, did all the homely and necessary offices for them which dainty and queasy stomachs cannot endure to hear named; and all this willingly and cheerfully, without any grudging in the least, showing herein their true love unto their friends and brethren; a rare example and worthy to be remembered.[23]

Bradford himself was among those who fell ill during this winter of testing. In particular, he singled out William Brewster and Myles Standish as two stalwarts who, preserved by God from sickness, labored with dedication to help others.

A common storehouse, twenty feet square, was built into which goods were moved from the Mayflower and some of the sick were housed there. On the night of January 14, a spark set the thatched roof on fire and the building was badly damaged before the fire could be extinguished. This was one more setback for the sick and for those whose personal property was stored there.

By March 21, the last of the Pilgrims had moved ashore from the Mayflower.

---

[23] Bradford, *Of Plymouth Plantation*, p. 77.

During February, Indians had been seen at a distance, but there had been no contact between the two peoples. Bradford wrote that about March 16, an Indian walked into the new village and greeted the Pilgrims in English. He gave his name as Samoset and requested beer from the astonished settlers. It turned out that he was a Pemaquid from what today is Maine who had learned his limited English from fishermen and traders. His love of travel had led him south and he had been living with the Wampanoags for several months.

Samoset introduced the Pilgrims to Squanto (or Tisquantum) who apparently was the only surviving Patuxet. He had traveled to England in 1605 with Captain George Weymouth who had explored the area where the Patuxets lived. He sailed back to his home with Captain John Smith who left Captain Thomas Hunt in command with orders to fill his ship with fish and furs before returning to England. Hunt, though, decided that slaves would be more profitable and seized twenty Patuxets, among whom was Squanto. Sold as a slave in Spain, Squanto served for a time in a monastery before escaping to England. In 1619, he came again to his home only to find the village empty, all having fallen victim to smallpox. He was taken in by the Wampanoags. As a result of his experiences, his English was better than that of Samoset. [24]

Relations between the Pilgrims and the Wampanoags now progressed to where the sachem (chief) Massasoit with twenty of his braves visited Plymouth. Edward Winslow, who was to develop as the chief diplomat of Plymouth both to the Indians and to England, stayed with the main body of the Wampanoags as a hostage. Massasoit was met by Myles Standish and a squad of armed men who escorted him and

---

[24] *Ibid.*, pp. 79-81.

his party to where they were greeted by Governor Carver, resplendent in his magistrate's robe and accompanied by drum and trumpet. Middle class commoners they may have been, but the Pilgrims, being Englishmen, knew how to put on a ceremonial show.[*] Squanto and Samoset served as translators at the conference which now ensued. Both sides agreed to a simple treaty of peace, punishment of those who broke this peace, and mutual defense.[25]

To make things even better, the winter, actually a rather mild one for the latitude, came to an end and spring reappeared.

> The spring now approaching, it pleased God the mortality began to cease amongst them, and the sick and lame recovered apace, which put as [it] were new life into them, though they had born their sad affliction with much patience and contentedness as I think any people could do. But it was the Lord which upheld them....[26]

Perhaps Bradford paused on a soft spring day to let the warmth of the sun and the smell of the earth and new life envelop him. Mixed with the sad recollections of his dead wife and of friends who did not survive the winter no doubt

---

[*] George Willison was in error when he stated of the Pilgrims that "The Forefathers were never ones for mummery and ceremonial. They had no use for precedent and tradition, and deliberately flouted both." (George F. Willison, *Saints and Strangers* [New York: Reynal and Hitchcock, 1945], p. 434.)

[25] Bradford, *Of Plymouth Plantation*, pp. 80-81.

[26] *Ibid.*, p. 84.

were the profound Christian faith which recognized that they would be reunited in heaven and the sheer joy of spring.

On April 5, the Mayflower set sail for England where she arrived on May 6, a voyage quicker and more pleasant than that of the previous autumn. It is significant to note that, in spite of the suffering of that first winter, not a single Pilgrim elected to return to England. These were tough, determined people who would not accept defeat.[*]

Also, with the coming of warmer weather, Squanto taught them to catch herring during their spring run and to use some of them to fertilize the mounds in which the corn was planted.

The joy over the coming of spring was tempered by sadness over the sudden death of Governor Carver. While working in the fields planting during a hot day in April, he was struck by what apparently was a cerebral hemorrhage and died a few days later. Elected to succeed him was William Bradford, thirty-one years of age, who was to serve in this post for all but five years until his death in 1657. Consistently the overwhelming choice of the Plymouth voters, he did successfully resist election these few times. Even then, though, he served as an assistant during the administrations of Edward Winslow and Thomas Prence.

The Pilgrims regarded the climate at Plymouth as similar to that of England, perhaps somewhat hotter in summer, a bit colder in winter, and without much fog. The soil was productive enough for them to grow the food they needed.

---

[*] Within the year, Captain Jones was dead, perhaps as a result of that hard winter at Plymouth, and after another year, the Mayflower, also worn out, had ended her career.

Fish, mussels, lobsters, wildfowl, and deer were abundant as were grapes, strawberries, gooseberries, and plums.[27]

The Pilgrims had learned of the Massachusetts tribe, a warlike people living not too far to the north on the shores of a large bay. Bradford determined to learn more of them, to explore the prospects for peace and trade. In September, an expedition of ten men commanded by Myles Standish and including Squanto and two other Indians, sailed north. They landed near what today is Boston. Squanto had warned that the Massachusetts were hostile, but Standish found them willing to trade.

Returning to Plymouth, Standish and the men who had been with him gave glowing reports of the Massachusetts Bay/Boston Harbor area. Edward Winslow was impressed especially by the potential harbors which he considered superior to Plymouth. Bradford, though, believed that God had led them to Plymouth, that the people had labored hard, and that prospects were good for a bountiful harvest. Furthermore, they had an alliance with Massasoit and the Wampanoags. All in all, most had bonded with their new home and were loath to pack up and move.[28]

As autumn approached, Bradford wrote of the Pilgrims that "they found the Lord to be with them in all their ways, and to bless their outgoings and incomings, for which let His holy name have the praise forever, to all posterity."[29] He also recorded that they had their health back, their homes were

---

[27] G. Mourt, *Mourt's Relation*, p. 84.

[28] Bradford, *Of Plymouth Plantation*, pp. 89-90; G. Mourt, *Mourt's Relation*, pp. 77-80.

[29] Bradford, *Of Plymouth Plantation*, pp. 89-90.

built, crops and fishing had been bountiful. Therefore, a time was set aside for giving thanks to God for His having preserved them through adversities and His meeting their needs.

Since the Indians had been so helpful, Massasoit was invited. He arrived with ninety braves, which must have been rather daunting to the people of the little colony. The Indians, however, killed and dressed five deer which they added to the wild turkeys and various vegetables from the gardens of Plymouth so that the repast was abundant and satisfying. Various sporting activities separated times of feasting over a three-day period. Any group of healthy young men (and even older ones) need to test themselves, so the reader readily can imagine contests of marksmanship with musket and bow, bouts of wrestling, and foot races. Good fellowship prevailed.[30]

The actual date is unknown, but the event gave rise to the annual day of Thanksgiving, one of the most beloved of American holidays.

It should be noted that the Pilgrims were not as dour, abstemious a lot as they often have been depicted. Although condemning drunkenness as contrary to Scriptural teachings, they did use alcoholic beverages such as beer and brandy in moderation. Furthermore, their clothing was not always as somber in color as frequently portrayed. On special occasions, Myles Standish wore a plum red cape and William Brewster an emerald green doublet.[31] Among items left by

---

[30] Letter by Edward Wilson to a friend in England, December 11, 1620, quoted in *Ibid.*, p. 90n.

[31] Peter Marshall and David Manuel, *The Light and The Glory* (Old Tappan, New Jersey: Fleming H. Revell Company, 1977), p. 128.

William Bradford at his death were a red Turkey grosgrain suit of clothes, and a red waistcoat and a "sad colored" suit, a "stuff suit with silver buttons," an "old violet colored cloak," and "two hats--a black one and a colored one."[32]

Just as all were feeling better about facing their second winter, in November the ship Fortune arrived from England with thirty-six new colonists, including Jonathan Brewster (eldest son of William Brewster) and Thomas Prence who later would serve as governor. The infusion of new settlers was welcome, but they arrived with no additional provisions. The colony's resources would be strained over the winter, but the Pilgrims accepted the situation with grace and tightened their belts.

Also arriving on the Fortune and rather more welcome was a patent brought by Robert Cushman from the Council For New England headed by Sir Ferdinando Gorges to whom King James in November 1620 had granted the territory between 40° and 48° north latitude, roughly from Philadelphia to Newfoundland. The patent was made out to John Pierce and his associates. He was a London merchant and close associate of Thomas Weston. The exact terms of the text are not known, but it did regularize the status of Plymouth.

In December, the Fortune left on her return voyage to England, braving the wintry north Atlantic since she was loaded with clapboards and beaver and other skins as a beginning return on the backers' investment in the colony. Sadly, though, she was captured by the French and the cargo seized, a financial setback for all. [33]

---

[32] Bradford, *Of Plymouth Plantation*, p. xxvi.

[33] *Ibid.*, pp. 92, 94, and 107.

The Pilgrims did reject frivolity on Sunday and when there was work to be done. Since they could find no Biblical date for Christmas, they did not celebrate December 25. Reinforcing their position was that the day had become a holiday with much drunken revelry in England. Bradford recorded that most of the newly arrived colonists refused to work on Christmas day, stating that to do so would violate their consciences. He responded that since they were new to Plymouth and its ways, he would excuse them this time. When Bradford and the other workers came back at noon, they found the excused playing various games in the street, whereupon he broke up the sport and informed them that it violated his conscience that some should play while others worked. Since that time, he observed wryly, "nothing hath been attempted that way, at least openly."[34] Here Bradford displayed his sense of humor along with a clear determination that no one would trifle with him or with the ways of Plymouth.

With the colony now settled, Bradford proposed by letter to Alice Southworth, widow of Edward Southworth, both of whom had been members of the Leyden congregation. She accepted and in 1623 arrived in Plymouth on the Anne together with her sons, Thomas and Constant. Shortly thereafter, she and Bradford were married. They had two sons, William and Joseph, and one daughter, Mercy. Information on Joseph and Mercy is sketchy. William, though, distinguished himself as assistant governor and treasurer of Plymouth, as a commissioner to the New England Confederation, and as a major in the Plymouth militia; he was wounded in action during King Philip's War.

---

[34] *Ibid.*, p. 97.

Bradford raised and educated his stepsons as his own. Each served as an assistant governor of the colony.

Little is known of John, Bradford's son by his first wife, Dorothy. He did come to Plymouth seven years after the Mayflower* and lived in Plymouth, Duxbury, Marshfield, and Norwich, Connecticut where he died in 1678.

---

* See p. 15, second footnote.

THE CHURCH

In the separatist congregational churches, the leaders were termed elders. Normally they were four in number. Two were ordained clergymen--the preaching elders or pastors and the teaching elders or teachers. The other two, ruling elders, were laymen. The pastors were to exhort the congregations and the teachers were to explain the Bible in a scholarly manner. Sometimes the teachers acquired more prestige, but the positions were intended to be equal and often distinctions between them became blurred.

On Sunday mornings, the beat of a drum summoned the people to the front of Captain Standish's home where they formed themselves three abreast and marched to church, the men fully armed and the governor wearing his robe of office.[35]

Typically the Pilgrims began their Sunday services at 8:00 a.m. The congregation stood for the opening prayer which continued for an hour or so. Then the pastor read and explained two or three chapters from the Bible. Next a psalm was sung without instrumental accompaniment. A sermon followed, lasting about two hours. Another psalm came after it. When Baptism or Holy Communion[*] were part of the service, they came now. After the collection and a closing prayer, the service ended about noon. A brief meal preceded the regathering of the congregation for what was termed "prophesying." Once the pastor or the teacher had read a

---

[35] George D. Langdon, Jr., *Pilgrim Colony: A History of New Plymouth 1621-1691* (New Haven, Connecticut: Yale University Press, 1966), p. 34.

[*] In Plymouth as well as in Boston, Holy Communion was celebrated using a chalice and real wine. Cyclone Covey, *The Gentle Radical: A Biography of Roger Williams* (New York: The Macmillan Company, 1966), p. 54.

passage from the Bible and had commented on it, the service was open for any other man who also wished to comment.[36]

Christians today, living in a more secular society in which Sunday has come to mean recreation and catching up on work, would find this a burden. So devout were most of the Pilgrims, though, that all this was joy to them.

Until 1624 there was no clergyman in Plymouth. John Robinson, the pastor at Leyden, had been expected to join the colonists, but, since the majority of his congregation had remained at Leyden, he believed that his place was with them. As a ruling elder, William Brewster could conduct services and preach, but was not permitted to administer the two sacraments--Baptism and Holy Communion. Probably his not having graduated from Cambridge precluded his being ordained by the church in Plymouth since the Pilgrims, although not well-schooled in a formal sense, did appreciate university educated men and required that background of those who served them as pastors and teachers.

In March 1624, the Rev. John Lyford, a priest in the Church of England, arrived at the insistence of the London backers. Initially he made a good impression on the settlers since he renounced his denominational ties. It appeared that he was moving to become one of them, although, still hoping that Robinson would cross the Atlantic, the church leaders refrained from ordaining Lyford. Although he held holy orders from the Church of England, the separatist congregationalists accepted no ordination, except their own.

Lyford, though, was an unstable double-dealer with real moral problems. When he first arrived, he displayed great

---

[36] Smith, *Bradford of Plymouth*, pp. 90-91.

humility and support for the Pilgrims' church. Bradford rather sarcastically recorded that tone:

When this man first came ashore, he saluted them with that reverence and humility as is seldom to be seen, and indeed made them ashamed, he so bowed and cringed unto them, and would have kissed their hands if they would have suffered him; yea, he wept and shed many tears, blessing God that had brought him to see their faces, and admiring the things they had done in their wants, etc., as if he had been made all of love and the humblest person in the world.[37]

In spite of all this, he allied himself with John Oldham and a small group of recalcitrant settlers who had arrived shortly before on the Anne and the Little James. These people had been recruited by the English financial backers of the colony and were not really in accord with the spiritual convictions of the Pilgrims. Although Lyford was treated well by the Pilgrims and accepted as a member of their church, he held Anglican services on the sly. Furthermore, he wrote letters back to England attacking the Plymouth leadership, letters which were intercepted by Bradford.

Confronted with this evidence of duplicity, Lyford confessed and abjectly begged forgiveness. He was sentenced to be exiled from Plymouth, the sentence being stayed for six months with the hope extended to him that if he truly reformed, it would be lifted. Once again, though, he reverted to form and was expelled early in 1625. Before the expulsion,

---

[37] Bradford, *Of Plymouth Plantation*, pp. 147-148.

his wife informed a deacon and several friends that Lyford had a record of adulteries.[38]

Once again, there was no pastor until 1628 when a Rev. Rogers served for one year. He was succeeded by Ralph Smith who pastored from 1629 until 1635. He did not prove to be a strong, successful holder of the post and his departure was not much lamented.[39]

The most successful clergyman to this point was to be John Rayner, a graduate of Cambridge who crossed the Atlantic in 1635 and served as teacher. Bradford referred to him as "an able and godly man ... of a meek and humble spirit, sound in the truth and every way unreproveable in his life and conversation." Yet even he left for unknown reasons in 1654 and moved to Dover, New Hampshire.[40]

Another Cambridge graduate, John Norton, spent four months as a teacher in the Plymouth church, but declined to stay as pastor. He accepted a call to pastor at Ipswich in Massachusetts Bay from whence he moved to First Church, Boston, succeeding John Cotton and becoming one of the most powerful clergymen in New England.

In 1638, the Rev. Charles Chauncy arrived to assist John Rayner in the Plymouth Church. A man with an impressive academic background, he had been a fellow and lecturer in Greek at Cambridge University. Bradford referred to him as "a reverend, godly and very learned man."[41] He soon caused contentions, however, by maintaining that the only proper

---

[38] Willison, *Saints and Strangers*, p. 251.

[39] Bradford, *Of Plymouth Plantation*, pp. 292-293.

[40] *Ibid.*, p. 293.

[41] *Ibid.*, p. 313.

means of baptism was by immersion. The Pilgrims accepted immersion, but did not mandate it, also believing sprinkling to be equally valid. The Plymouth leaders were willing to put up with Chauncy's views if he were willing to accept those who differed with him and baptized by sprinkling. This he would not do. The dispute was sent to churches in Massachusetts Bay, Connecticut, and New Haven for their conclusions. They too opposed Chauncy who left in 1641 for Massachusetts Bay where, as might have been expected, he again stirred up strife with his pronouncements. In 1654, his learning, though, led to his being elected president of Harvard College with the proviso that he keep his position on baptism to himself. Apparently he regarded this opportunity as worth the price of circumspection and accepted the terms and the office.[42]

Most intriguing of all the Plymouth clergymen was Roger Williams who spent somewhat over two years there during his rather peripatetic career. Relatively little is known of his early years. His own writings do not shed much light on the subject, due partially to his own reticence when it came to writing of himself and partially to the fact that all surviving records from his pen, with the exception of a few letters, were produced after his thought had developed and matured, none coming from his formative years.

It is known that Williams was born into a middle class family. His mother's family had emerged from obscurity during the reign of Elizabeth, advancing into the ranks of the lesser landed gentry. His father was a London shopkeeper of comfortable means, a member of the Merchant Taylors at a time when the wealth, prestige, and power of the guilds were declining before the onslaught of the joint stock companies.

---

[42] *Ibid.*, pp. 313-314.

During the time of Williams' childhood, Puritan reformist spirit, both within and without the Church of England, was spreading rapidly through the realm and possibly may have been a factor in St. Sepulchre's, the home parish of his family.

Under normal circumstances at that time, a young man of the middle burgher class would not have been able to gain a university education. Williams, however, had the excellent fortune to attract the attention of the eminent jurist Sir Edward Coke who sponsored him as a student at Charterhouse School and Pembroke Hall, Cambridge. He received his B.A. in 1627 and remained for two more years of advanced study in theology following which he was ordained a priest in the Church of England. Soon, however, his views became markedly Separatist and he left the Church. In 1630, he accepted an invitation to minister in the new Massachusetts Bay colony.

Almost immediately he clashed with Governor Winthrop and the leaders of the Boston Church by rejecting the post of teacher in that church when it was offered to him and by refusing to receive Holy Communion with them "because I durst not officiate to an unseparated people, as upon examination I found them to be."[43] He argued that the people would have to repent publicly for their having received Communion in Church of England parishes before coming to New England. Williams believed that the Church of England had retained too many Roman Catholic ways and it did not require a Christian conversion experience for membership. Favorable reputation for piety and scholarship plus a

[43] Edmund S. Morgan, *Roger Williams: The Church and the State* (New York: Harcourt, Brace and World, Inc., 1967), p. 25.

charming personality he may have had, but this was hardly getting started on the right foot.

In April, though, Williams was called by the Salem Church to be an assistant to the sickly pastor, Samuel Skelton. This, as might be expected, was opposed vehemently by the leadership of the colony, although neither the government nor any other church had any jurisdiction over the decisions of the local congregations. The constant confrontations became so aggravating to Williams that he determined to move to Plymouth where he would be among a separated people. This he did in late 1631 or early 1632.

Here he was welcomed, his reputation having preceded him, and served as the teacher of the Plymouth Church although he was not officially inducted as such. William Bradford, normally a good judge of people, wrote the following:

> Mr. Roger Williams, a man godly and zealous, having many precious parts but very unsettled in judgment, came over first to the Massachusetts; but upon some discontent left that place and came hither, where he was friendly entertained according to their poor ability, and exercised his gifts amongst them and after some time was admitted a member of the church. And his teachings well approved, for the benefit whereof I still bless God and am thankful to him even for his sharpest admonitions and reproofs so far as they agree with truth.[44]

Bradford too had a charitable streak, but the irrepressible Williams would sorely strain it. Even in Plymouth, more tolerant and closer to his beliefs on separation, he was to stir

---

[44] Bradford, *Of Plymouth Plantation*, p. 257.

controversy. He came to see an incomplete separation. For example, when some members of the church visited back in England, they attended Church of England services, but were not expelled from the Plymouth Church upon their return. This, he believed, tainted the Plymouth Church and would taint him too were he to remain.

His demand for total separation was not all, though; he proceeded to question enforcing religious precepts with the power of the civil government. Williams concluded that there is no basis in Scripture for this practice. He struck at the very foundation of the Pilgrim/Puritan position by arguing that although Israel was truly a covenanted people, this relationship was abrogated with the Resurrection of Christ and that until His Second Coming and the end of this world order, there would be no nation, no government, no people which would exist in an organizationally covenanted relationship with God. Civil governments had been ordained by God for the maintenance of civil law and order.

> That in these late years God has made it evident that
> all civil magistracy in the world is merely and
> essentially civil. And that the civil magistrate can
> truly take cognizance of nothing as a civil magistrate
> but what is proper and within his civil sphere.[45]

The Old Testament Israel was not to be used as a literal guide for the manner in which contemporary governments should be conducted since it was a type of the true Israel, the spiritual Church of Jesus Christ. Since this is a spiritual body, it cannot be identified with any religious organization. If no

---

[45] Roger Williams, *Limits of the Civil Magistrate*, in Irwin H. Polishook, ed., *Roger Williams, John Cotton and Religious Freedom* (Englewood Cliffs, New Jersey: Prentice-Hall, Inc., 1967), p. 62.

specific church in the world can be identified with the Church of Christ, the case against the state's enforcing religious precepts becomes even stronger. The church and the state must be separate. The Pilgrims agreed in part with Williams, but he went beyond where they were prepared to go; his rejection of the covenant relationship with God and his call for total toleration were too much for them.* All things considered, it became increasingly obvious to Williams and the Plymouth leadership that his stay in the colony was not working out.

In 1633, he accepted a call from the Salem Church and returned to Massachusetts Bay for a second round. Once again, contentions ensued. Williams attacked the charter of the colony, arguing that no European monarch had the right to award land in the New World, that it could be acquired legitimately only by purchase from the Indians. He further averred that magistrates should not administer oaths to unregenerate individuals since this therefore required them to make false statements. He also demanded that the churches completely separate themselves from the Church of England at a time when they were attempting to go their own way in effect while keeping a technical tie so as to avoid antagonizing Charles I. All this culminated in his expulsion from Massachusetts Bay in 1635 and his founding Rhode Island.

Quakers made only limited penetration of Plymouth prior to the death of Bradford in 1657. Shortly before, a couple of complaints came out of Sandwich. In one, two women were accused of creating a disturbance during a worship service. The second involved several people who were accused of

---

* See pp. 46-47.

holding meetings in a home on Sundays at which they denounced the church and the government of the colony. Seventeenth century Quakers often were fiery protesters who vociferously demanded change in church and state. For example, they rejected the organized church, would not take oaths, and refused military service. Although Plymouth was more tolerant than Massachusetts Bay where four Quakers were hanged after repeatedly breaking laws against their activities, still there they were fined, whipped, and one even exiled.[46] Once again, the Pilgrims, lovers of freedom though they were, placed their concern for the establishment of a Biblical commonwealth as they saw it on a higher level.

In 1616, a group of Englishmen in London founded the first church to designate itself "Congregational." For fear of the authorities, worship services were held secretly, this being the England of James I. John Lothrop, an alumnus of Cambridge University and formerly a priest in the Church of England, became their pastor in 1624. Having been caught at worship, Lothrop and forty-two others were imprisoned in 1632. Released two years later, he and thirty members of his congregation crossed the Atlantic to Plymouth colony, settling in Scituate. In 1639, Lothrop with most of his people moved to Barnstable* where they remained. In 1717, they started construction of the West Parish Meetinghouse. This congregation today is the oldest continuously meeting

---

[46] Eugene Aubrey Stratton, *Plymouth Colony: Its History and People 1620-1691* (Salt Lake City: Ancestry Publishing, 1986), pp. 90-91.

* See p. 43n.

Congregational Church in the world and their building is the oldest Congregational Church structure in the United States.[47]

Their church was central to the lives of the settlers of Plymouth. After all, these people went through the pain, struggle, and turmoil of being a spurned minority in England, exiles in the Netherlands, and colonists in the New World because of their deep Christian faith, including their conviction that separatist congregationalism was the true Biblical path. They believed that each congregation should be independent, that no bishops or presbyteries should exercise jurisdiction. A general accord united the clergy and people of the different congregations in the colony, but there was no governing authority above the local church. Whether one agrees or disagrees with this conclusion pales into insignificance before the widespread respect for their faith, integrity, courage, and hard work. Familiar even to children are pictures of Pilgrim families heading to church on Sunday morning with Bibles and muskets, a vivid depiction of Charles Kingsley's ideal of muscular Christianity.

Pastors never had the influence in Plymouth that they had in Massachusetts Bay where they were the most dominant force. To an extent, this was due to the circumstance of doing without a pastor for a number of years and without one they liked for even more years. A more significant factor, though, was the nature of the Pilgrims. They were devoutly Christian and determined to establish a Christian commonwealth; they respected clergy whom they found worthy and appreciated the preaching and teaching of the Bible and the administration of Baptism and Holy

---

[47] Historical brochure published by the West Parish Meetinghouse, West Barnstable, Massachusetts.

Communion. They were, though, an independent-minded lot who rejected clericalism and strongly espoused the importance of the laity.

In contrast to the state churches of Europe, no one automatically was a member of one of the churches of Plymouth simply by virtue of living within the borders of the colony. Church membership here was limited to those who made a profession of faith and who demonstrated that faith through good behavior. Apparently the Pilgrims at some point in time increased the strictness of their admissions standards, adding the requirement that prospective members must testify to their having had a salvation experience. This may have been brought in during the Bradford years. It was mentioned in 1679 by the younger John Cotton, pastor of the Plymouth Church.[48] There is no definite proof as to whether the added proviso started with the Plymouth Church, then moved out from there, or whether it began with the Massachusetts Bay Puritans, as Edmund Morgan suspects.[49]

Marriages were performed by civil magistrates since the Pilgrims could find no Biblical warrant for ministers to perform them.[50] They also rejected any religious ceremonial when someone died. Their concern was lest funeral services lead to praying for the dead and burning candles for them, practices the Pilgrims associated with the Roman Catholic doctrine of purgatory.[51] Since the Pilgrims were determined

---

[48] Edmund S. Morgan, *Visible Saints: The History of a Puritan Idea* (New York: New York University Press, 1963), pp. 61-62.

[49] *Ibid.*, pp. 65-66.

[50] Bradford, *Of Plymouth Plantation*, p. 86.

[51] Willison, *Saints and Strangers*, p. 480.

to build a Christian commonwealth, they were not dealing with the contemporary liberal view separating church and state in terms of separating the sacred from the secular as competing belief systems. Institutionally they were separate; leaders did not hold office in both. For example, when John Done was chosen to be a deacon, he resigned as an assistant to the governor.[52] But, the leaders in the government were church members, so there was no cleavage between them. A civil marriage was performed by a Christian man.

The first marriage in Plymouth, performed by Gov. Bradford, was in 1621, joining Edward Winslow, whose wife had died two months previously, and Susanna White, a widow of three months with two children.[53] Lest the haste in their marrying appear unseemly, it must be remembered that the Pilgrims were struggling for survival in primitive frontier conditions and that families were essential, not only for spiritual and moral nurturing, but also for cooperative work in providing food, clothing, and shelter. Although the short-lived communal economy still had a couple more years to run, it definitely was not to the Pilgrims' liking. Since they rejected the Scylla and Charybdis of communalism and radical individualism, the intact family had to flourish along with the church to provide the social framework within which individuals could grow, develop, and express themselves.

Under Plymouth law, divorces were granted for adultery, bigamy and willful desertion.[54] Overall, substantial protection

---

[52] Smith, *Bradford of Plymouth*, p. 219.

[53] Willison, *The Pilgrim Reader*, p. 149.

[54] Demos, *A Little Commonwealth: Family Life in Plymouth Colony*, pp. 92-93, 96-97.

was provided for women. For example, husbands were punished through the legal system for abusing their wives and wronged wives did receive favorable settlements.[55]

---

[55] *Ibid.*, pp. 93-95, 97.

GOVERNMENT

When William Bradford was elected governor in April 1621, one assistant was selected to serve under him. In 1624, because of the increase in governmental responsibilities, Bradford called for four more assistants. This was done. Two more were added in 1633. The governor and the seven assistants formed the General Court which combined executive, legislative and judicial functions.

As the colony grew, new towns were established. Plymouth the town increasingly was distinguished from Plymouth the colony and a separate local government developed. During the 1630s, Duxbury, Scituate, Taunton, Sandwich, Barnstable, and Yarmouth were organized.* Representative government would develop to replace the annual meeting of the freemen at Plymouth. In 1637, the General Court was reorganized to have five delegates from Plymouth and two each from the other towns in addition to the governor and the assistants.

In 1630, Isaac Allerton returned to Plymouth from England with a patent from the Council for New England signed by Sir Ferdinando Gorges and the Earl of Warwick granting to Plymouth the territory south and east of a line running along the south shore of Boston Bay to the head of Narragansett Bay and widened the colony's holdings on the Kennebec. The patent designated William Bradford as the trustee for the colony, technically making it his. The territory

---

* The dates of incorporation for towns were: Plymouth, 1620; Scituate, 1636; Duxbury, 1637, Barnstable, 1639; Taunton, 1639; Sandwich, 1639; Yarmouth, 1639; Marshfield, 1641; Rehoboth, 1645; Eastham, 1646; Bridgewater, 1656; Dartmouth, 1664; Swansea, 1667; Middleborough, 1669; Edgartown, 1671; Tisbury, 1671; Little Compton, 1682; Freetown, 1683; Rochester, 1686; Falmouth, 1686; and Nantucket, 1687. (Demos, *A Little Commonwealth: Family Life in Plymouth Colony*, p. 11).

was granted to "William Bradford, his heirs, associates and assigns."[56] He took the Purchasers* in with him as his associates. They considered themselves to be trustees for all rather than as an elite lording it over the lesser beings.

This was not to be a permanent status. Bradford did not seek personal power and gain, but rather the welfare of the colony; he had no intention of having it remain in effect his personal estate. By the end of the decade, the economic status of Plymouth had improved. In 1640, the General Court voted to pay the Purchasers £300 and to approve of their retaining some land for themselves. In return, Bradford and the Purchasers would surrender the patent. In 1641, the agreement was culminated. Bradford and his associates turned over to "the Freemen of this Corporation of New Plymouth, all that other right and title, power, authority, privileges, immunities and freedoms granted in the said Letters Patents by the said Right Honourable Council for New England."[57]

Because of a glitch in the negotiations in England, the patent did not have the Great Seal and so Plymouth did not have a royal charter, something which added to their weaknesses when confronting the growing power of Massachusetts Bay.[58]

Expansion of the colony also necessitated a more developed judiciary. With the division into three counties in

---

[56] Bradford, *Of Plymouth Plantation*, p. 429n.

* They were men who in 1627 joined together to retire the debt of the colony. See pp. 58-59.

[57] *Ibid.*, p. 430.

[58] Willison, *Saints and Strangers*, p. 287.

1685, judicial organization took its final form. At the top was the Court of Assistants which sat three times per year in Plymouth. Magistrates and associates for county courts were chosen by the General Court. Selectmen's courts had jurisdiction over all routine matters in the towns.[59]

The General Court, including the governor, and local officials, were chosen in annual elections by the freemen-- adult male heads of households. Unlike in Massachusetts Bay, church membership was not required for freeman[*] status, but anyone settling in Plymouth had to be approved by the governor or by two of the assistants. Later, the leaders in the towns became the determining factors in these decisions. About 50% of the adult males in Plymouth qualified for the franchise, a percentage that would not be equaled in England until the latter part of the 19th century. For example, in 1643 there were 634 males subject to militia duty, meaning they were between 16 and 60. At the same time, 234 were classified as freemen.[60] Subtracting those under 21, the number of adults was about 50%.

In 1672, after the death of Bradford, a property requirement was added as a prerequisite for holding freeman status.

---

[59] Herbert L. Osgood, *The American Colonies in the Seventeenth Century*, Vol. I: *The Chartered Colonies. Beginnings of Self-Government* (Gloucester, Massachusetts: Peter Smith, 1957), pp. 297-298.

[*] The black population of Plymouth cannot be ascertained with any degree of certainty. There were some black indentured servants, possibly a few slaves, but the trend definitely was to freedom as indicated in probate records. Some were freemen. Stratton, *Plymouth Colony*, pp. 187-189.

[60] Morison, "The Pilgrim Fathers in History," p. 238.

The Pilgrims considered uniformity of religious belief to be necessary for good civic order. They did not, however, regard themselves as the only Christians and reject all others.

For example, in spite of substantial differences with Roman Catholicism, they were hospitable to individuals of that faith. In late 1650, Father Gabriel Druillettes, a Jesuit missionary to the Abenaki Indians of Maine, came south to Plymouth from the Kennebec where he had become friendly with John Winslow (brother of Edward) who ran the Plymouth trading post there. Bradford received him hospitably at a time when it was a capital offense in England to have dealings with Roman Catholics. He even demonstrated respect for their practices by serving fish at his first meal with Druillettes, it being a Friday.[61]

Still, though, there were limits beyond which most of the key leaders were not prepared to go. A proposal presented to the General Court in 1645 to extend full toleration to all who would be peaceable and obey the laws had a considerable amount of support. This would cover not just various varieties of Christians, but non-Christians as well. This represented the thought of William Vassall who had arrived in Massachusetts Bay with Winthrop and had become an important member of the colonial government. He came to oppose the Puritan establishment on the issue of tolerating religious dissent. He returned to England, then in 1635 came back to the New World, settling in the town of Scituate in Plymouth. Here he again advocated expanding toleration, gaining the support of prominent Pilgrims such as Timothy Hatherly, Edmund Freeman, John Browne, and Myles

---

[61] Smith, *Bradford of Plymouth*, pp. 307-308; Thomas J. Fleming, *One Small Candle: The Pilgrims' First Year in America* (New York: W. W. Norton and Company, Inc., 1964), p. 179.

Standish. Opposing the proposed change were William Bradford, Thomas Prence, Edward Winslow, and William Collier who believed that such a blanket policy would lead to civil confusion and chaos. Through parliamentary maneuvering, the idea was blocked and died in the General Court.[62]

Yet Plymouth under Bradford was quite tolerant in practice when measured by the standards of the day. Quakers in the colony never were executed, branded, beaten, had their ears cut off, or their property confiscated as was done in Massachusetts Bay. But, as the years passed, Bradford died, a new generation arose, and more religious diversity developed, the power of government came to be used more to keep things from changing too much. In 1657, a law was passed against Quakers and other "heretics" and in 1659 six Quakers were banished. Even after Bradford, though, Plymouth never became as restrictive as most other European and colonial political jurisdictions of the seventeenth century. For example, records show that in 1670 several members of the Swansea Baptist Church were freemen.[63]

The laws of Plymouth were simpler than those of England. At that time English law imposed the death penalty for a multitude of offenses whereas Plymouth cut the number to seven--treason, murder, witchcraft, adultery, rape, sodomy, and arson. During the history of the colony, executions were carried out only for murder and sodomy.[64]

---

[62] Willison, *The Pilgrim Reader*, pp. 494-495.

[63] Langdon, *Pilgrim Colony: A History of New Plymouth 1620-1691*, p. 82.

[64] Willison, *Saints and Strangers*, p. 319.

John Billington, one of the original Mayflower settlers, had caused frequent trouble during the next decade.[65] It all came to a head in 1630 when he ambushed John Newcomen, with whom he had quarreled, and mortally wounded him. Billington was arraigned by a grand jury and tried before a jury of his peers. He was convicted and sentenced to death. Uncertain of their authority to execute, Plymouth inquired of Governor John Winthrop of Massachusetts Bay who concurred with the sentence. Billington was duly hanged.[66]

Demonstrating the determination of Bradford to ensure justice for all people of Plymouth, Indian as well as English, was the execution of three settlers in 1638 for murdering an Indian. A Narragansett who had been in Massachusetts Bay trading, as he returned to tribal lands, passed into Plymouth territory where he fell in with Arthur Peach, Thomas Jackson, Richard Stinnings, and Daniel Cross. Peach, the ringleader, was described by Bradford as a man who had served capably in the Pequot War, but now was an out-of-work, dissolute troublemaker.[67] He lured the Indian to sit down with him and his friends, then ran him through with a rapier, robbed him, and left him for dead. The Indian, though mortally wounded, made it across the border to Rhode Island. Before dying, he identified his attackers not only to fellow Narragansetts, but also to Roger Williams, the founder of the colony, and to Dr. Thomas Jones who treated him. Cross escaped, but the others were captured. Since the crime had taken place in Plymouth, they were tried there. Found guilty, they were executed in

---

[65] Bradford, *Of Plymouth Plantation*, pp. 156, 234.

[66] *Ibid.*, p. 234.

[67] *Ibid.*, p. 299.

spite of some sentiment that no Englishman should be put to death for killing an Indian.[68] This sort of thinking, though, would not prevail in the Plymouth of William Bradford.

The sodomy case involved bestiality by a young man named Thomas Granger who was observed having sexual relations with animals and confessed. He was indicted, tried, and sentenced to death. In accordance with Leviticus 20:15, the animals were slain and then Granger was executed on September 8, 1642.[69]

The gravity of this violation led Bradford to reflect upon how this could have happened in a colony founded by Christians upon Christian principles. He observed that when the Lord's work is being done, Satan will oppose and attempt to thwart these endeavors. He further commented that everyone who came to Plymouth was not spiritually and morally sound. Sometimes people see believers being blessed in a material sense and join them for outward reasons as the Israelites attracted a "mixed multitude" when God afflicted the Egyptians and led His people out of Egypt, this being recorded in Exodus 12. He further stated that some who proved to be troublesome were sent by friends who hoped that the Godly influence of the Pilgrims would improve them. Others simply wanted to get rid of burdens or shame. Bradford did concede that some Pilgrims, desiring workers, were not sufficiently discerning about the servants they engaged.[70]

---

[68] *Ibid.*, pp. 300-301.

[69] *Ibid.*, p. 320.

[70] *Ibid.*, pp. 321-322.

In a broader sense than this particular crime, Bradford reflected that there had been in Plymouth cases of drunkenness and sexual immorality. He observed that the power of the Holy Spirit is required to restrain human lusts. When people do not restrain themselves because of their commitment to Biblical morality but are restrained by strict laws, they chafe under them, and then burst forth violently against them.

> Another reason may be, that it may be in this case as it is with waters when their streams are stopped or dammed up. When they get passage they flow with more violence and make more noise and disturbance than when they are suffered to run quietly in their own channels; so wickedness being here stopped by strict laws, and the same more nearly looked into so as it cannot run in a common road of liberty as it would and is inclined, it searches everywhere and at last breaks out where it gets vent.[71]

As can be seen from this passage, Bradford had a sense of perspective about Plymouth, concluding that the colony was not worse than other societies, indeed no doubt was better, but that here standards were higher and immorality noticed more.

> A third reason may be, here (as I am verily persuaded) is not more evils in this kind, nor nothing near so many by proportion as in other places; but they are here more discovered and seen and made public by due search, inquisition and due punishment; for the churches look narrowly to their

---

[71] *Ibid.*, pp. 316-317.

members, and the magistrates over all, more strictly than in other places.[72]

Bradford may not have been university educated, but he obviously was impressively self-educated through wide reading and was an astute observer of human nature. Time and again he impresses the reader with his strength and firmness of purpose together with a sensitive understanding of human weakness.

During the history of Plymouth Colony, only two witchcraft cases occurred, both after Bradford's death, and neither resulted in conviction. In 1661, Dinah Silvester of Marshfield accused the wife of William Holmes, claiming that she assumed the form of a bear. Mrs. Holmes was found innocent. Now her accuser was convicted of defamation and compelled to make a public apology. In 1677, Mary Ingham of Scituate was indicted for having bewitched Mehitable Woodworth, but was acquitted of the charge. Christian faith in Plymouth was deep and sincere, but not given to excesses.[73]

Often servitude was used as a means of punishment for petty crimes. For example, in 1644 James Till was found guilty of theft and was sentenced to serve the household of Timothy Hatherly for a period of two years.[74] Whipping and time in the stocks too were used for non-capital crimes.

---

[72] *Ibid.*, p. 317.

[73] Demos, *A Little Commonwealth: Family Life in Plymouth Colony*, p. 83, n. 1.

[74] *Ibid.*, p. 70.

EDUCATION

When Elizabeth I came to the throne in 1558, many schools had been closed because the monasteries and chantries which ran them had been dissolved by her father, Henry VIII. After a couple of decades, interest in and support of education increased. Hundreds of little primary schools, termed "petties," were opened. Children in the counties entered at about the age of six. These were not government schools, but were privately endowed with scholarships provided for students from poor families. Church of England clergy, both Puritan and more regular establishment types, provided much of the impetus behind this movement. Formal schooling for girls did not extend beyond the petties.

From about ages eight to fourteen, some students went on to grammar schools where the solid classical education for which England has become renowned was inculcated. In these schools, students from different social classes were mixed.

Approximately 2% matriculated at Oxford or Cambridge. Most of the others became apprentices, the sons of the gentry to rich, powerful merchants, those from lower classes to tradesmen and craftsmen.[75]

An area where Plymouth was weak in comparison with Massachusetts Bay was education. The Puritan colony to the north established its first Latin grammar school* in 1635. The next year, Harvard College was founded. A 1647 law required all towns with fifty or more freeholders to appoint a

---

[75] Francis Dillon, *The Pilgrims* (Garden City, New York: Doubleday and Company, Inc., 1975), pp. 31-32.

* The term refers to secondary schools which emphasize college preparatory courses.

teacher and all towns with one hundred or more freeholders must have a Latin grammar school. Plymouth, though, did not set up its first public school until 1671.[76] This slowness was more a reflection of the smaller number of university educated people and the lower economic status of the English Separatists who founded Plymouth compared with the Massachusetts Bay Puritans than it was an indication of little interest in education by all in Plymouth, although, admittedly, such interest was greater in the colony to the north. Plymouth was less prosperous and fewer educated people emigrated there. Still, some families did provide private instructions for their children, a few banding together to hire a teacher. William Bradford provided a program in politics and public administration for his sons, stepsons, and nephews.[77] Only a few of the better off families were involved. For most inhabitants of Plymouth, education was sketchy.

The General Court in 1663 recommended that there be a schoolmaster in each town. In 1671, the government collected money for Cape Cod fishing rights and used the funds to establish a school open to all while charging a small fee. Initially, many of the people in the colony did not have much interest in higher education, being satisfied if young people could read the Bible, write, and do basic arithmetic.[78]

Furthermore, in keeping with English society of that time, education was for boys; most of the Plymouth women were

---

[76] Herbert Eugene Bolton and Thomas Maitland Marshall, *The Colonization of North America 1492-1783* (New York: The Macmillan Company, 1920), p. 220.

[77] Willison, *Saints and Strangers*, pp. 384-385.

[78] *Ibid.*, p. 387.

not literate, Bradford's second wife, Alice, and Bridget Fuller, wife of Samuel, being among the few exceptions. In fact, over a century would pass before the first school for girls would open in Plymouth.[79]

---

[79] Willison, *Saints and Strangers*, p. 387.

THE ECONOMY

Bradford Smith wrote in his biography of William Bradford that the Pilgrims developed "a classless society in an era of rigid class distinctions."[80] While it is true that they did not transplant the English class system to the New World, they had clear leaders in the church, in government, in the military, and in the economy. The clergy, the higher officials of the colony, and the richest farmers were classified as gentry, even though they had not enjoyed that status back in England. They were addressed as "Mr.," pronounced "master," and their wives as "Mrs.," or "Mistress." Yeomen and husbandmen, those who owned and farmed their own land, were called "goodman," their wives "goodwife," sometimes shortened to "goody."[81] Furthermore, Plymouth tax records showed variations in tax rates based on variations in wealth.[82] Since the people of Plymouth were free to achieve or not to achieve, a class system emerged naturally, albeit one which was more mobile than that of England and one which did not have the wide variation of status found there. By no means were they a bunch of Levelers committed to equality of condition, but rather people more attuned to the natural aristocracy views later expounded by Edmund Burke and John Adams.

Less than a month after the first Thanksgiving, Robert Cushman, a deacon in the church, gave a sermon, "The Danger of Self Love," in which he warned the Pilgrims not to believe that they were entitled to God's bounty because of what they had done to earn it. He also warned them not to

---

[80] Smith, *Bradford of Plymouth*, p. 10.

[81] Stratton, *Plymouth Colony*, p. 213.

[82] *Ibid.*, pp. 48-49.

give in to competing with one another in the accumulation of worldly goods. Just as Satan sinned and fell by wanting to be superior to his fellow angels, indeed, even equal to God, so too this worldliness can separate people from God.[83]

By and large, the generation of Plymouth founders lived by this admonition. Although no great wealth was generated by any entrepreneur of this colony, there were those who were quite comfortable, men such as William Bradford, yet they never made worldly goods the focus of their lives.

The policy of economic communalism imposed at the beginning of the colony led to serious problems when implemented at Plymouth. No one could own private property, with the exception of some personal items. Since the fruits of all labor went into the common treasury, everyone was on the same level; the energetic and the sluggish were treated the same. Incentives to work hard and to be productive were limited.

In the spring of 1623, Bradford faced the prospect of another planting season and harvest less productive than they should have been with several more of the same until the seven years mandated in the original contract had been fulfilled. Also a number of the settlers asked him to permit people to work for themselves on their own land and pay a tax on their proceeds. Understanding that he was violating the agreement with the English backers, Bradford took upon himself the responsibility for ending this wrongheaded policy. He determined to assign land to each family in proportion to its size. Each would be responsible for its

---

[83] Arthur Quinn, *A New World: An Epic of Colonial America from the Founding of Jamestown to the Fall of Quebec* (New York: Berkley Books, 1994), pp. 101-102.

sustenance and permitted to reap the benefits of its labor. For a few more years, cattle would be owned jointly and Bradford organized several companies of men to keep the only fishing boat active on a regular basis, but no longer would the heavy hand of communalism bear down on Plymouth, stifling productive enterprise. The colony would practice Christian charity and access to water, fishing, and fowling would be open to all, but there would be no acceptance of the belief that everyone had an equal right to everyone else's labor. Bradford criticized the view of Plato "and other ancients applauded by some of the later times; that the taking away of property and bringing in community into a commonwealth would make them happy and flourishing; as if they were wiser than God."[84]

Responding to those who argued that the communal principle was right, but failed because of the decadent nature of the people, Bradford stated that: "Let none object this is men's corruption, and nothing to the course itself. I answer, seeing all men have this corruption in them, God in His wisdom saw another course fitter for them."[85]

With this insight into human nature, Bradford foreshadowed Adam Smith. Because of human fallibility, it is better to have economic freedom so that those who wish to succeed in the long run must focus on providing for others quality products, reasonable prices, and good service. Negative traits are channeled, at least outwardly, by the desire to succeed. Voluntary cooperation by all parties is

---

[84] Bradford, *Of Plymouth Plantation*, pp. 120-121.

[85] *Ibid.*, p. 121.

fostered. While no economic system can guarantee that virtue will prevail, a free market does promote good more effectively and minimize bad better than the alternatives. Still, as will be seen, Plymouth would not develop a totally laissez-faire system.

Relations between the London merchant backers and the colonists were constantly strained. It was understandable that both sides were dissatisfied. The merchants were disappointed in the return they were receiving on their investment while the settlers in Plymouth believed they were working hard, doing all they could in the face of many tribulations. In 1627, a way out for both sides was negotiated. The previous year, Isaac Allerton* had crossed to England. Early in 1627, he returned to Plymouth with an offer from the London merchants to sell all their claims for £1800. In addition, there was a debt of £600.

By this time, the population of Plymouth had grown only to 180 people. Since few settlers had much money, it was clear that the burden of settling the debt could not be shared by many. There was also concern that the debt burden would discourage the settlers from raising funds to provide for more immigration from Leyden. The solution was for eight men in Plymouth and four in London to assume the debt. The eight, known as the "Undertakers," were: William Bradford, Myles

---

* Allerton proved to be an erratic financial agent for Plymouth in England, sometimes capable, often incompetent, sometimes perhaps crooked. The exact nature of his machinations is not really clear from records. Bradford did refer to Allerton's having cheated William Brewster, whose daughter he had married. (Bradford, *Of Plymouth Plantation*, p. 242). He also referred to his being greedy (*Ibid.*, p. 239). Apparently he mixed his personal business arrangements with those of the colony, generally losing money. He again returned to Plymouth in 1630 with the charter (see pp. 43-44), but left for good in 1633. After more years of fruitless speculation and scheming, he died insolvent (Dillon, *The Pilgrims*, pp. 204-205).

Standish, Isaac Allerton, Edward Winslow, William Brewster, John Howland, John Alden, and Thomas Prence. Associated with them in London were: John Sherley, John Beauchamp, Richard Andrews, and Timothy Hatherley[*].

In return, these men would have a monopoly on the Indian trade for six years. Plymouth men established trading posts at Aptucxet on Cape Cod, in Maine on the Penobscot and Kennebec Rivers, and on the Connecticut River north of Hartford. They were quite successful in trading with Indians for beaver, otter, and mink pelts. After the six years had passed, the monopoly would lapse.

The Undertakers brought into association with them heads of families and single men in order to organize better the trade of the colony and the retiring of the debt. Each man received one share and each head of family an additional share for other members of the household. Those joining in this joint stock operation were known as "Purchasers" or "Old Comers."[86]

Furthermore, in 1627 joint ownership of livestock was ended. Since there were not enough animals in the colony at that time for there to be distribution to each family, the colonists were divided into twelve companies, each of which received one cow and two goats. In January 1628, some land which had not yet been divided was allocated by lot.

In reference to the economy, Isaack de Rasieres,[**] Secretary of New Netherland, after his 1627 visit, wrote that the soil was stony, making the farms less prosperous than

---

[*] Later he emigrated to Plymouth.

[86] Osgood, *The Chartered Colonies. Beginnings of Self-Government*, pp. 117-118.

[**] See pp. 81-82.

those of New Netherland. Fish and birds were abundant. He wrote also of the successful fur trade.[87]

John Pory,* an epicure of large girth, was enthusiastic about the availability of fish, fowl, and various types of berries. Bluefish and lobsters especially delighted him. He found the people healthy.[88]

Emmanuel Altham was a member of the gentry class whose family had numerous ties to law and commerce. A younger son, he inherited little from his parents' estate and, as was typical for younger sons, he had to plot his own course if he wanted success. Opportunities for wealth and excitement beyond English shores attracted him. He invested in the Company of Adventurers for New Plymouth and served as company agent. He came to admire the Pilgrims and became fascinated by the prospects for New England development. Although interested in making money for himself and for the company, Altham more than anything else was caught up in the romance and challenge of colonization. In particular, his admiration for the Plymouth colonists was deep. His letters reflected his own devout Christian faith.**

---

[87] Sidney V. James, Jr., ed., *Three Visitors to Early Plymouth* (Bedford, Massachusetts: Applewood Books, 1997), pp. 75-80.

* See p. 80-81.

[88] James, ed., *Three Visitors to Early Plymouth*, pp. 75-80.

** Apparently, though, either he became disappointed after three years of experiences with Plymouth or he became restless for new adventures, for he joined the East India Company in 1626. He served in India with distinction as a soldier and enjoyed success in business as well. He returned to England, but died shortly thereafter in 1636.

In 1623, he sailed to Plymouth as captain of the Little James, a forty-four ton pinnace* which was to be used for fishing, in the fur trade, and even for a spot of privateering. Writing to his brother, Sir Edward Altham that same year,

he stated that Plymouth was well situated on a hill close to the ocean with a good harbor. He said that the town had about twenty houses, "four or five of which are very fair and pleasant, and the rest (as time will serve) shall be made better."[89] He too was impressed by the military preparedness--the fort, the artillery there, and the eight-foot high palisade surrounding the community.[90]

Altham considered the economic prospects of the colony to be promising with fish abundant and wild fowl plentiful. At the time he wrote, the fur trade was developing well. He also anticipated impressive profits from timber, which he said was as good as any he had ever seen.[91] He recommended the development of saltmaking. Although this was done, it never became significant during the years that Plymouth was a separate colony.**

---

* A pinnace is a small vessel, generally two masted and schooner-rigged.

[89] James, ed., *Three Visitors to Early Plymouth*, p. 24.

[90] *Ibid.*

[91] *Ibid.*, pp. 26-28.

** At first, sea water was boiled in large iron kettles. Then the salt was scraped off after the water had boiled away. This was a process which produced meager results. In the next century, large shallow troughs and evaporation come into use. With more sophisticated methods and greater demand, saltmaking became a good moneymaker by the nineteenth century. (Henry C. Kittredge, *Cape Cod: Its People and Their History* [Boston: Houghton Mifflin Company, 1968], pp. 150-154.)

Still Plymouth never became a very prosperous colony. Although most of the people were hardworking and there was no grinding poverty, wealth did not develop there as it did to the north in Massachusetts Bay. A number of factors accounted for this difference. As was stated earlier, the Massachusetts Puritans were not separatists as were the settlers of Plymouth. In England, separatists were fewer in number and had less wealth at their disposal. Consequently, Massachusetts Bay had more people from its inception and it was better financed. Furthermore, Boston harbor was far better for extensive trade than was the shallower harbor at Plymouth.

From the arrival of John Winthrop in 1630 with over 1,000 people, Massachusetts Bay was substantially larger in population. By that year, Plymouth only numbered about 250. That figure increased to about 1,800 in 1643 and 5,000 in 1675. Just before Plymouth ceased to be a separate colony in 1692, its population was somewhat over 10,000. Massachusetts Bay, though, grew more rapidly and by the end of the century was the most populous of the English colonies with 80,000 people.[92]

The soil at Plymouth was not rich, precluding the development of a thriving agrarian society. Although some surplus corn was produced for export, farming generally was for subsistence. Fish were abundant in New England waters, but the Pilgrims never derived much economic success from fishing, perhaps because of a shortage of money for

---

[92] Darrett B. Rutman, *Husbandmen of Plymouth: Farms and Villages in the Old Colony, 1620-1692* (Boston: Beacon Press, 1967), pp. 13, 15, and 21. Samuel Eliot Morison, *The Oxford History of the American People* (New York: Oxford University Press, 1965), p. 131.

investment in boats, perhaps because few of them were comfortable at sea.

Another problem faced by the Pilgrims during this vexing time was a devastating hurricane which hit in August 1635. Bradford wrote that it began shortly before dawn, not increasing in stages as is the common pattern, but striking suddenly. Many homes were destroyed or damaged seriously, trees were torn up by the roots or snapped off in the middle. The full force continued about five or six hours, leaving behind extensive destruction and memories not soon forgotten.[93]

There was some export of clapboards and a limited extraction of salt from ocean water, but the fur trade was the best of the at best modest economic enterprises at Plymouth. Their traders ranged from Long Island to Maine and, as previously stated,[*] established trading posts on the Connecticut River near Hartford, at Aptucxet on Cape Cod near where the Cape Cod Canal[**] now runs, and in Maine on the Kennebec River and at Penobscot near the present town of Castine.

Plymouth's fur trade was to fade, though, due to population growth along the Connecticut and the emergence

---

[93] Bradford, *Of Plymouth Plantation*, pp. 279-280.

[*] See p. 59.

[**] The narrow neck of Cape Cod was almost cut through by the Manomet River which ran out into Buzzards Bay and Scusset Creek which flowed into Cape Cod Bay. In 1676, Samuel Sewall wrote of the feasibility of a canal which would improve coastal trade by eliminating the necessity for the dangerous voyage around the Cape. Finally, the canal was dug and opened to traffic in 1914.

of a separate colony there and the harsher reality of the
French seizure of Penobscot in 1635.

Growing internal strife between King Charles I and
Parliament precluded help from the home government.
Charles was determined to avoid war so that he would not
have to go to Parliament for funds and be faced with a quid
pro quo which would increase their power. By the latter years
of the century, the long duel between England and France for
control of North America would begin, culminating in the
English victory at Quebec in 1761 and the expulsion of France
from North America except for the small islands of St. Pierre
and Miquelon.

The capitalism of Plymouth was tempered by the
conviction that the reality of the sin nature necessitated a
degree of governmental supervision over some aspects of
economic enterprise lest human frailty lead to a decline of
Christian love before the onslaught of material greed. Goods
made in Plymouth were subjected to standards. Coopers had
to make their barrels tight and according to the standard
measurement used in London. Dissatisfaction with the
quality of iron produced at the Taunton ironworks resulted in
an order to correct the deficiency.[94]

In 1635, the General Court of Plymouth empowered the
governor and the assistants to control prices and wages. For
example, Thomas Clark paid a thirty shilling fine for having
bought a pair of boots and spurs for ten shillings and having
sold them for fifteen shillings.[95] To encourage development,
sometimes towns subsidized the building of gristmills and

---

[94] Langdon, *Pilgrim Colony*, p. 149.

[95] *Ibid.*, p. 148.

herring weirs. Under these circumstances, prices were set. Also, at one time, the government sold authorization to seine fish at Cape Cod for a set number of years and applied the money to support elementary schools.[96]

This policy did not continue long, however. It collapsed before the dual assault of the theoretical--a growing conviction that honest business profits did not contravene Scripture--and the practical--the inability of the small colony to develop the bureaucracy necessary to maintain price and wage controls. Increasingly in Plymouth, as well as in Massachusetts Bay, free market economics were seen to be the right course for a Christian society, with, of course, honesty expected and enforced, a conclusion foreshadowed by Bradford's statements.[*]

Between 1631 and 1636, over £10,000 worth of beaver and other skins were shipped to England, consigned to James Sherley. He was to pay the debts of Plymouth from the proceeds, but he did not do so. He was fired and sued, but the debt remained. The Plymouth Undertakers now determined to pay off everything. In order to retire it once and for all, Bradford and several others sold some of their own holdings.[97]

In Plymouth, contrary to England at that time, women could inherit property and enter into contracts, such as between a widow and a new prospective husband prior to their marriage. Sometimes women were granted liquor

---

[96] *Ibid.*, p. 149.

[*] See p. 57.

[97] Langdon, *Pilgrim Colony*, p. 33.

licenses. The records of the colony are not clear in reference to other types of business activities by women.[98]

Furthermore, in another departure from English practice, Plymouth law struck down primogeniture, stipulating that all children of a marriage would be heirs to land, not just the eldest son.[99]

---

[98] Demos, *A Little Commonwealth: Family Life in Plymouth Colony*, p. 90.

[99] Dillon, *The Pilgrims*, p. 223.

INDIANS

Historians often comment on the divergent views of property held by Europeans and Indians, remarking that the former believed that when they negotiated for the purchase of land, that it became theirs just as was true in England whereas the Indians believed that they were selling the right to use the land, not the exclusive possession of it. While that may be true, the Indians did understand change of possession by military conquest. Frequently among the Indian tribes, the powerful killed, enslaved, or drove out the weaker, taking over their lands. This treatment was not inflicted on the Indians by the Plymouth of William Bradford. They were not displaced from their land by force and the Gospel was presented to them.

Emmanuel Altham* arrived in Plymouth in 1623. Struck by the good relations between the colonists and the Indians, Altham reported that Massasoit attended Bradford's wedding with his primary wife and about 120 warriors. He also brought several deer and a turkey.

He also stated that when the Indians arrived, "we saluted them with the shooting off of many muskets and training our men."[100] No doubt this reflected a ceremonial welcome, but also was a friendly reminder of the military prowess of the Plymouth militia. Probably the 120 braves accompanying Massasoit too served both a ceremonial purpose and as a show of strength. Bradford and Massasoit may have been friends, but it is quite likely that each wanted the other to keep in mind the strength he could marshal.

Altham was impressed by Massasoit. He wrote:

---

* See pp. 60-61.

[100] James, ed., *Three Visitors to Early Plymouth*, p. 29.

And now to speak somewhat of Massasoit's stature. He is as proper a man as ever was seen in this country, and very courageous. He is very subtle for a savage, and he goes like the rest of his men, all naked but only a black wolf skin he wears upon his shoulder. And about the breadth of a span he wears beads about his middle.[101]

During 1621, Hobomok, one of Massasoit's key Councilors, came into Plymouth where he remained until his death. He served as a representative of the Wampanoags during his years there. He became particularly close to Myles Standish, becoming a rival to Squanto who was associated more with William Bradford. This rivalry was fostered by the leaders of Plymouth as a means of learning more, of being more likely to get important intelligence information to guide them in their Indian policy.

One day during the summer, Hobomok came to Bradford with the report that he and Squanto had been attacked by Corbitant (Cauntabant), sachem of the Pocassets, because they were friendly with the colonists. Bradford called together his close supporters and decided that Standish would take fourteen men to Nemasket, now Middleborough, where they were to determine the fate of Squanto. If the reports of Squanto's death were true, they were to behead Corbitant. Possibly Bradford was part of the force because that would have been consistent with his temperament and only about twenty able-bodied men were left in Plymouth at that time. The attack was successful, Squanto was fine, and Corbitant escaped. This show of resolve impressed other

---

[101] *Ibid.*, p. 30.

Indians who professed their peaceful intentions. Even Corbitant later made his peace with Plymouth.[102]

Squanto too was capable of machinations, attempting to stir up trouble between Plymouth and Massasoit so as to enhance his own position. He also seems to have been bribed by the Indians to use his influence to keep the Pilgrims from unleashing the plague which he claimed they kept buried in the ground. Figuring out what Squanto had been up to, Massasoit demanded that he be turned over to him. Bradford managed, barely, to keep both the peace and Squanto's hide intact until the latter died of natural causes not long after.[103]

The Pilgrim attitude toward Indians was rather ambivalent. One the one hand, they saw themselves corresponding to the Old Testament Israelites, God's people occupying a land inhabited by non-believers. On the other hand, they were aware of the Great Commission which mandated to Christians:

> Go ye, therefore, and teach all nations, baptizing them
> in the name of the Father, and of the Son, and of the
> Holy Spirit,
>
> Teaching them to observe all things whatsoever I
> have commanded you; and, lo, I am with you always,
> even unto the end of the age. Amen.[104]

Edward Winslow, for example, talked enthusiastically of "converting them [the Indians] to the true knowledge and

---

[102] Bradford, *Of Plymouth Plantation*, pp. 88-89.

[103] *Ibid.*, pp. 98-99.

[104] Matthew 28:19-20.

worship of the living God, and so consequently the salvation of their souls by the merits of Jesus Christ. . . ."[105] This he wrote in 1623 in the Dedication to his brief history covering 1622-1623. Winslow developed substantial knowledge of Indian culture and languages and served Plymouth effectively as an emissary to them.

The missionary efforts of the seventeenth century settlers of Plymouth and Massachusetts Bay were, allowing for population differences, comparable in effectiveness to those of the Spanish in California.[106] Still, though, the Plymouth Church and separatists in general at that time tended to focus more on feeding and edifying Christians than on reaching out to the unconverted.

Squanto, apparently, was one of the first, if not the first, to convert. In the early autumn of 1622, he served as guide and interpreter for a trading expedition going down to Cape Cod. Both Bradford and Standish were part of this party. Squanto fell ill of a fever, so the Pilgrims put into Pleasant Bay which today is bordered by Orleans and Chatham. Bradford, perhaps troubled that the colonists had not done more to spread Christianity to the Indians, must have presented the Gospel message to Squanto who now, facing death, asked Bradford "to pray for him that he might go to the Englishmen's God in Heaven."[107] This sounds rather

[105] Edward Winslow, *Winslow's Relation: Good Newes from New England* (Bedford: Massachusetts: Applewood Books, no date given), p. 3. This book was published initially in England in 1624.

[106] Lloyd C. M. Hare, *Thomas Mayhew, Patriarch to the Indians (1593-1682)* (New York: AMS Press, 1964), pp. 201-202.

[107] Bradford, *Of Plymouth Plantation*, pp. 113-114.

spiritually rudimentary, but hopefully Squanto's faith was sound and he is together in heaven with his Pilgrim friends.

The Rev. John Eliot of Roxbury in Massachusetts Bay devoted himself to spreading Christianity to the Indians. He studied the language and translated parts of Scripture, such as the Lord's Prayer and the Ten Commandments. Entering Plymouth, he continued his ministry in Yarmouth and other parts of Cape Cod.

Especially significant was Richard Bourne, a well-to-do layman from Sandwich. He determined not just to convert the Indians to Christianity, but also to further their civic development and thereby to enhance their prospects for surviving as a people forming a part of the Plymouth colony. In 1660, they received from the colonial government title to fifty square miles at Mashpee. By five years later the community was established with its own courts and other organs of local government.[108]

Yet Bourne's primary focus was on the spiritual welfare of these people. He had four Indian preachers assisting him in his work which was successful since he reported that all the Mashpee Indians, between four and five hundred, became Christians. In 1670, he was ordained formally and continued to serve until his death in 1685.[109]

A younger contemporary was Samuel Treat who graduated from Harvard in 1669 and in 1672 was called to minister at Eastham, taking responsibility for Cape Cod below Yarmouth. Included in his ministry were both Europeans and Indians. As did Bourne, Treat trained and

---

[108] Kittredge, *Cape Cod: Its People and Their History*, p. 43.

[109] *Ibid.*, p. 44.

used Indian preachers and teachers. His work too was successful, the number of Christian Indians in his territory increasing from 300 to 500 over a twenty year period.[110]

Thomas Mayhew and Thomas Mayhew, Jr. undertook missionary work on Martha's Vineyard, moving there from Massachusetts Bay shortly after the first settlement was established at Great Harbor, now Edgartown, in 1642. Several generations of the family continued the missionary tradition.[111]

As a result of these efforts, villages of "Praying Indians" were formed on Martha's Vineyard, Nantucket, in Plymouth, and in Massachusetts Bay. For these Christian Indians, progress was slow in their movement toward a more advanced civilization. They were to suffer greatly at the hands of non-Christian Indians during King Philip's War.

Most of the Indian converts to Christianity in Plymouth were among the members of the small, fragmented tribes of Cape Cod. In other parts of the colony, success was more limited. Massasoit, although a firm friend of the Pilgrims, resisted conversion and blocked missionary activity among the Wampanoags.[112] On one dramatic occasion, he welcomed their medical ministrations if not their faith.

In March 1623, news arrived in Plymouth that Massasoit was gravely ill. At the same time, word also came that a Dutch ship had been driven ashore by a storm near his lodge. Bradford ordered Edward Winslow to take some medicine to treat Massasoit and to confer with the Dutch. The next day,

[110] *Ibid.*, p. 45.

[111] Hare, *Thomas Mayhew, Patriarch to the Indians (1593-1682)*, pp. 65, 76, 86.

[112] Willison, *Saints and Strangers*, pp. 389-390.

Winslow set off with Hobomok and an Englishman who had wintered in Plymouth. While on their way, they received information that Massasoit had died and that the Dutch ship had been re-floated--hardly an auspicious beginning to the mission. Since Corbitant,* sachem of the Pocassets, subject to the jurisdiction of Massasoit, was likely to succeed him, the Pilgrim party decided that it would be impolitic not to visit the prospective successor.

Corbitant was known to be considerably less enthusiastic about the Pilgrims than was Massasoit, so Winslow the diplomat hoped to improve relations. They missed Corbitant who was not in his village when they arrived, but they were informed, to their pleasant surprise, that Massasoit still lived.

When they arrived at Massasoit's village, Winslow found him in great distress, having lost his sight from some unspecified ailment. Upon further examination, Winslow learned that he had not had a bowel movement for five days and had not slept for two days. Furthermore, his jaws were almost locked together, although Winslow was able to get some of what he referred to as "a confection of comfortable conserves"[113] into the patient's mouth on the point of a knife. When he finally got Massasoit's mouth open, he found it heavily furred and his tongue badly swollen. Winslow cleaned out Massasoit's mouth and scraped his tongue, stating that he "got abundance of corruption out of the same."[114] After receiving more of Winslow's concoction (of which we know nothing) and drinking some water with

---

* See pp. 68-69.

[113] Winslow, *Good Newes from New England*, p. 34.

[114] *Ibid.*

more of this medicine in it, Massasoit's sight returned. The next day, he ate solid food, consumed a broth of strawberry leaves and sassafras root made up by Winslow, moved his bowels, and proceeded to give thanks to God and to Winslow for his recovery.[115]

While it probably is too dramatic to state that Winslow stood to lose his life had Massasoit died, still it is not impossible that such could have happened and Plymouth been attacked. It is not possible to know how the Wampanoags would have reacted had their chief died under the ministrations of a Pilgrim, nor is it possible to know if Corbitant would have been as implacable an enemy as was Massasoit's son Philip (or Metacom) who became sachem when his father did die in 1661. By then, Plymouth and the other English colonies in New England were quite powerful. In 1623, a smaller Plymouth would have been virtually alone. Providentially Massasoit lived in 1623 and the Pilgrims were blessed by almost forty years of peace with their closest Indian neighbors.

---

[115] *Ibid.*, pp. 31-35.

THE PEQUOT WAR

The first serious conflict between the British in New England and the Indians was the Pequot War of 1636-1637. A few years prior, the warlike Pequots* had penetrated into this region, becoming the dominant power between Narragansett Bay and the Hudson and incurring the enmity of those tribes whom they dominated--the Narragansetts, the Mohegans (or Mohicans), and the Niantics. At roughly the same time as their incursion was the northward and eastward movement of the Dutch who had settled in New Amsterdam (later New York) and the Hudson River Valley and the westward push of British settlements from the Atlantic coast. The expansion of vigorous, aggressive people into the same area was bound to lead to conflict; it remained for some incident to ignite it.

Earlier in the 1630s, the governments of Plymouth and Massachusetts Bay had discussed their cooperating in the development of trade along the Connecticut River. Governor Winthrop of Massachusetts Bay declined, stating that hostile Indians and rivers unsuited to easy trade made the proposal unappealing, but that there would be no objection if Plymouth went ahead on its own.

Meanwhile, in 1633 the Dutch established a small fort at what today is Hartford. Men from Plymouth passed the position, ignoring Dutch threats to fire upon them, and built their own fort to the north.

In the spring of 1634, a smallpox epidemic decimated the Indians of the area. Bradford wrote movingly and graphically of the suffering of the Indians and of the efforts by the English to aid them in spite of the fear of infection. Yet, as he stated:

---

* The name means "destroyers."

But by the marvelous goodness and providence of God, not one of the English was so much as sick or in the least measure tainted with this disease, though they daily did these offices for them for many weeks together. And this mercy which they showed them was kindly taken and thankfully acknowledged of all the Indians that knew or heard of the same.[116]

Upon learning of the reduced number of Indians and of the increasingly successful trade, men from Massachusetts Bay now arrived. Under William Brewster's son Jonathan, the Plymouth post on the Connecticut had been returning a good profit. John Oldham* and ten other men from Massachusetts Bay established a settlement they named Wethersfield, a short distance south of the Dutch fort. The growing numbers of people from Massachusetts Bay led to trouble with those from Plymouth over land which had been purchased from the Indians by the latter and into which the former were moving. Plymouth, a smaller, weaker, poorer colony had to give way. An agreement was reached according to which Plymouth recouped the money paid for the land and retained the trading post and one sixteenth of the land. The men from Massachusetts Bay received another one sixteenth and the remainder went to a group from Dorchester in Massachusetts Bay which had feuded with the Puritan leadership in Boston. They became the nucleus of the new colony of Connecticut.[117] Keeping Plymouth from being absorbed by the larger

---

[116] Bradford, *Of Plymouth Plantation*, p. 271.

* This was the same John Oldham who had caused trouble in Plymouth earlier. See p. 31.

[117] Smith, *Bradford of Plymouth*, pp. 256-259.

Massachusetts Bay would require considerable strength and skill from Bradford.

In 1636, John Oldham was murdered by Indians, possibly Narragansetts, at Block Island, who then were sheltered by the Pequots. Another trader from Massachusetts Bay, John Gallup, exchanged fire with Indians on board Oldham's captured ship off Block Island. The Massachusetts Bay government mounted a punitive expedition under Captain John Endecott. They struck Block Island, inflicting heavy casualties before crossing to the mainland where they burned several Pequot villages. They never did catch the actual murderers.

The Pequots, unsuccessful in forming alliances with other tribes because of resentment of their domination, launched their own attack against the English late in 1636. Led by their sachem (chief) Sassacus, they besieged Fort Saybrook near the mouth of the Connecticut River during that winter. In the spring they struck Wethersfield further to the north. Although they inflicted moderate losses on the settlers, the Pequots were unable to capture either location.

The Connecticut General Court now determined upon war and assigned Captain John Mason, a veteran of European conflicts, a force of ninety men for the campaign. They were joined by a contingent of Mohegans. Moving south from Hartford to Fort Saybrook, they skirmished with Pequots along the way. At Fort Saybrook, they were joined by a unit of forty men, soon reinforced by another one hundred, from Massachusetts Bay commanded by Captain John Underhill. The combined force now moved east by boat into Narragansett Bay where they landed and headed west overland to strike from an unexpected direction the main Pequot village which was located between the Mystic and

Thames Rivers. The attack on May 25, 1637 was successful. After an initial repulse, the colonial forces and their allies routed the Pequots and destroyed their village. In July, the last large group of Pequot warriors was routed in a battle a few miles from New Haven where they had been found hiding in a swamp.

Sassacus and a few other Pequots escaped westward and northward into the country of the Mohawks, one of the member tribes of the Iroquois Confederacy, where they were beheaded, an indication of hatred of the Pequots, a desire to show goodwill to the English,[*] and a determination to secure a large amount of wampum carried by Sassacus. Surviving Pequots were sold into slavery in Bermuda or were enslaved by their enemies the Mohegans, the Narragansetts, and the Niantics.

Troops from Plymouth did not participate in the war. Bradford wrote that the General Court voted to send fifty men, but that just as they were to set out, word arrived that the war was almost over and that there was no need for them.[118]

---

[*] Alliances between the British government and the Iroquois would continue through the American Revolution.

[118] Bradford, *Of Plymouth Plantation*, p. 295.

DEFENSE

Good relations between Plymouth and the Wampanoags continued through the life of Bradford (he died in 1657) until the death of Massasoit in 1661. He was succeeded by his vehemently anti-English son Metacom, better known historically as King Philip, the man who started King Philip's War, 1675-1676, a bloody conflict which resulted in the breaking of Indian power in eastern New England.

The Wampanoags, however, were not the only Indians. In January 1622, a Narragansett brave delivered to the Pilgrims an attempt at intimidation in the form of a bundle of arrows wrapped in a snakeskin.

Conanacus (or Cononicus), sachem of the Narragansetts, was hostile to the Pilgrims probably because of their alliance with Massasoit, his enemy. Exactly what they wanted is not clear from historical records, but that it was a threat and a challenge was very clear. Bradford stuffed the snakeskin with musket balls and returned it with the rejoinder "that if they had rather war than peace, they might begin when they would; they had done them no wrong, neither did they fear them or should they find them unprovided."[119] He understood that peace is not secured merely by hoping for it, but though Christian lover of peace he may be, still a firm stand for right and justice was called for and that his responsibility was to protect the freedom of Plymouth. Sometimes violence cannot be avoided, indeed is necessary in opposing evil. This sort of action by Godly governments is explained as follows:

> For rulers are not a cause of fear for good behavior,
> but for evil. Do you want to have no fear of authority?

---

[119] Bradford, *Of Plymouth Plantation*, p. 96.

Do what is good and you will have praise from the same; for it is a minister of God to you for good. But if you do what is evil, be afraid; for it does not bear the sword for nothing; for it is a minister of God, an avenger who brings wrath upon the one who practices evil.[120]

Continuing Bradford's policy of peace through strength, during the summer of 1622, a fort was built on the hill above Plymouth Harbor, the Pilgrims having learned of the deadly Indian attacks in Virginia. There was a naive segment of the population who argued that since peace then prevailed, the expense and labor were unnecessary. The majority, though, had the good sense to reject that fallacy.

The Pilgrims reflected the English principle that all able-bodied men should be trained and prepared to defend the realm. Englishmen of that time served in the militia from the age of sixteen until they were sixty. The training was rudimentary, but it did at least provide basic instruction in weapons handling and in military formations. In 1634, Plymouth passed a law which made all men "subject to such military order for trayning and exercise of arms as shall be thought meet, agreed on, and prescribed by the Governor and assistants."[121]

In the late summer of 1622, John Pory, Secretary of the Virginia Colony, visited Plymouth on his way back to England. An accomplished scholar and an experienced

---

[120] Romans 13:3-4.

[121] Douglas Edward Leach, *Arms For Empire: A Military History of the British Colonies in North America, 1607-1763* (New York: The Macmillan Company, 1973), p. 11.

traveler, he was a keen observer of the new settlement, observations he recorded in correspondence to Henry Wriothesley, Earl of Southampton, who was Treasurer (chief executive) of the Virginia Company. He commended the Pilgrims for their military preparedness, as exemplified by the fort and the palisade around the settlement, and for their firm attitude toward the Indians demonstrated by their handling of the threat from Corbitant[*][122] He further said of the Pilgrims that "because as they never did wrong to any Indians, so will they put up no injury at their hands. And though they gave them kind entertainment, yet stand they day and night precisely upon their guard."[123] Again clearly displayed was their desire for peace combined with the willingness by the people of Plymouth to fight if necessary to preserve their lives, their families, their way of life, an attitude reflecting the prayerful vigilance precedent of Nehemiah: "Nevertheless, we made our prayer unto our God, and set a watch against them day and night...."[124]

Isaack de Rasieres, Secretary of New Netherland, visited Plymouth in 1627. He presented his impressions of the new English colony in a letter to Samuel Blommaert, a prominent Dutch merchant and a director of the West India Company. Although there was some rivalry between the home countries and some problems along the Connecticut River where spheres of influence overlapped, relations between the two colonies were to be good. They shared a similar faith and

---

[*] See pp. 68-69, 73.

[122] James, *Three Visitors to Early Plymouth*, pp. 11-12.

[123] *Ibid.*, p. 12.

[124] Nehemiah 4:9.

generally were not rivals for the same territory or trading areas.

In his letter, de Rasieres described the town of New Plymouth as being on the slope of a hill rising from a sheltered bay. A broad street ran from the shore up the hill to a large square fort at the top which had six cannons on the upper level from which the surrounding countryside could be commanded. The lower level was used for church services. A second street intersected the first at a 90° angle halfway up the hill. Here, at the intersection, was Governor Bradford's home. Also at the intersection were mounted four guns which could enfilade the streets. A stockade surrounded the town with gates at the ends of the streets.[125]

Prior to King Philip's War (1675-1676), the most commonly used firearm was the matchlock which was fired by a slow-burning match-cord which had been soaked in saltpeter. It was so heavy that it had to be rested on a forked stick when being fired.[126] This weapon was awkward, slow, and not dependable in bad weather. From the beginning of the New England colonies, the more reliable flintlocks were in use and became more common each decade. In these weapons, the gunpowder was ignited by a spark produced when the trigger was pulled, causing a flint to strike against steel. The typical flintlock musket was ¾" bore, 3½'-4½' long, and weighed fourteen or fifteen pounds. Individual targets could be hit at eighty to one hundred yards and volley fire at

[125] J. Franklin Jameson, ed. *Narratives of New Netherland 1609-1664* (New York: Charles Scribner's Sons, 1909), pp. 111-112.

[126] Osgood, *The Chartered Colonies. Beginnings of Self-Government*, pp. 501-502.

opposing units was effective at one hundred fifty to two hundred yards.[127]

The Plymouth militia, commanded by Myles Standish, was divided into four units of infantry, one of which was led by Bradford. In 1658, the first troop of cavalry was organized in the colony. Initially consisting of 33 men, it later was increased to 48. Once the men were inducted, their horses were no longer considered taxable property. In 1675, the troopers were ordered to acquire carbines and to serve as dragoons (mounted infantry). They refused to do so, were disbanded and were reassigned to infantry companies.[128]

The Plymouth militia units mustered for training at least six times per year. The men provided their own weapons. In each town, all able-bodied freemen of good reputation who had been approved by the officers and the majority of the company were inducted. Each session opened and closed with prayer. Annually, when company officers were elected, a sermon was preached.[129]

Well aware of history and the dangers of military domination of government, the people of Plymouth, indeed of all the English colonies, were determined to maintain control of the military by the civil government. This worked well in a society in which the leaders in all areas--church, government, military, business--shared the same spiritual, moral, and political convictions. The officers and soldiers of the militia companies were an integral part of the community; they did not form a separate class. This is an important point to be kept in mind constantly by those who

---

[127] Leach, *Arms For Empire*, pp. 4-6.

[128] Osgood, *The Chartered Colonies. Beginnings of Self-Government*, p. 505.

[129] *Ibid*., pp. 507-508.

wish to remain free from internal oppression and safe from outside threats.

TROUBLESOME NEIGHBORS

Thomas Weston*, having broken with the Pilgrims and their London bankers, decided to launch a colonization project of his own. In 1622, a company of about fifty commanded by his brother Andrew, landed at Plymouth where they definitely were not welcome. The Westons were regarded as unreliable, unscrupulous scoundrels. All were provided for, however, until they moved north to Wessagusset, today Weymouth, where they built a settlement. They turned out to be more schemers and dreamers than workers; planting and fishing languished and little fur trading was done. Furthermore, they cheated Indians and stole from them.

Apparently Indians, led by Wituwamat of the Massachusetts tribe, determined to strike at Wessagusset and, knowing that the Weston Company had lived in Plymouth for a time, decided to attack there also. From their friend Massasoit, the Pilgrims learned of the plot and that the Nauset, Cummaquid, Manomet, Pamet, and Gay Head tribes had been recruited. To preempt Wituwamat, Myles Standish was sent to Wessagusset with a contingent of the Plymouth militia. Wituwamat and a group of his followers came into town and he contemptuously boasted of the English and French he had killed. A short time later, Standish and his men attacked, killing Wituwamat and two other braves in hand-to-hand combat. The other Indians in the settlement were seized and the Pilgrim contingent moved out of town and encountered another force of the Massachusetts tribe which

---

* See p. 5.

they routed. This decisive action deterred other Indians, nipping in the bud the whole plot.[130]

After going through a hard winter, the settlers of Wessagusset had had enough of pioneering and abandoned the settlement.

In 1623, Captain Robert Gorges, son of Sir Ferdinando Gorges, arrived, determined to make a go of the Wessagusset settlement now that the Weston colonists had thrown in the towel. Even more significant was his having a commission from the Council for New England to be governor of the region, including Plymouth. Bradford would move from being governor to being a member of the Council. After experiencing the vicissitudes of New England colonial life, especially the winter, Gorges lost interest in the whole matter and returned to England. Plymouth continued to control its own affairs.[131]

Just northwest of Wessagusset, a group led by Captain Wollaston established Passonagessit, now Braintree, in 1625. Two years later, Wollaston moved on. Stepping forward to lead the remnant was Thomas Morton, a lawyer of the gentry class who had arrived with Wollaston. Charles Andrews referred to him as "a bohemian, a humorist, a scoffer, and a libertine with no moral standards of thought or conduct."[132] Conversely, Willison considered him to have been a cultured, well-educated man unjustly maligned by Bradford and the

---

[130] Willison, *Saints and Strangers*, pp. 215-229.

[131] Bradford, *Of Plymouth Plantation*, pp. 133-138; Willison, *Saints and Strangers*, pp. 238-239.

[132] Charles M. Andrews, *The Colonial Period of American History, Vol. I: The Settlements* (New Haven, Connecticut: Yale University Press, 1964), p. 333.

Pilgrims.[133] The subsequent history of the settlement gave credence to Andrews.

Morton renamed the settlement Mare Mount--Mountain by the Sea. Either deliberately or mistakenly the Pilgrims called it Merry Mount and so it generally is called by historians. Apparently licentiousness involving whites and Indians, men and women was widespread. Also, Morton and his people traded firearms and alcohol to the Indians. Finally, competition between Plymouth and Merry Mount for the fur trade became intense. Evidence seems to indicate that the Plymouth concerns were legitimate, motivated by more than jealousy over fur trade rivalry. A combination of moral anarchy, alcohol, and firearms certainly would diminish prospects for civilized order in the region. Although it was not under the jurisdiction of Plymouth, it represented too great a threat to ignore.

Plymouth gained support from some other settlements in 1628 (Massachusetts Bay had not yet been established) to take action against Merry Mount. Again Myles Standish commanded the unit which seized it without any Plymouth casualties and only one injury among the defenders. Morton was exiled to England in spite of the demand by Standish that he be executed. He continued an enemy of the Pilgrims, writing against them and seeking to have their patent revoked.[134]

---

[133] Willison, *Saints and Strangers*, p. 274.

[134] Bradford, *Of Plymouth Plantation*, pp. 204-210; Willison, *Saints and Strangers*, pp. 275-284.

MASSACHUSETTS BAY

To the north of Plymouth, the Massachusetts Bay Colony was founded, enjoying advantages over its neighbor from the very beginning. It represented the vision of English Puritans, people who wanted to change the Church of England from within rather than separate from it as had the Pilgrims. They wanted to remove vestiges of Roman practice, such as most clerical vestments, using the sign of the Cross in Baptism, kneeling to receive Holy Communion, and the episcopal form of church government. The Puritans were more in number with more wealth and more education than were the Separatists. This resulted in considerably more backing for Massachusetts Bay than Plymouth could hope for.

Puritan colonization began in 1623 at Cape Ann followed by a settlement at Salem in 1626. In 1629, the Massachusetts Bay Company was set up with a royal charter. The next year, John Winthrop arrived with over 1,000 people and Boston was established as the capital of the colony. Winthrop, a member of the gentry class, had been educated at Cambridge, studied law at Gray's Inn, and had achieved prominence as an attorney and as a justice of the peace.

During the spring of 1629, John Endecott, then the governor of Massachusetts Bay, wrote Bradford requesting medical assistance because of sickness among settlers recently arrived from England. Endecott had heard of the reputation of Samuel Fuller, erstwhile serge maker in Leyden who was a deacon in the Plymouth Church and functioned as the colony's physician. Bradford agreed to the request and Fuller duly sailed north to Salem where he helped medically and conferred with the Puritans on church organization. They had much in common in spite of the latter's determination at that time to remain within the Church of

England. The next summer, he and Edward Winslow, Plymouth's prime diplomat, again went to Massachusetts to discuss church matters.[135] Relations between the two colonies were off to a good start, but this was not to last; breakers lay ahead.

In September 1630, a vessel set sail from Salem to trade with the Indians on Cape Cod. It was forced by weather to take shelter in Plymouth Harbor. Learning of the trading plan, the Pilgrims vehemently objected to this rejection of their jurisdiction over the Cape. Bradford wrote a stinging note of protest to Massachusetts Bay, asserting that Plymouth was prepared to fight, if necessary, to defend their land. Bradford then determined to meet personally with Winthrop in view of the earlier warm relations between the colonies. Each was favorably impressed by the other and a solid friendship developed based on common Christian faith*, although the Massachusetts Bay Puritans were to disappoint Bradford by not becoming full-fledged separatists, and on mutual respect.

During the autumn of 1632, Winthrop led to Plymouth a delegation which included the Rev. John Wilson of the Boston Church and Captain John Endecott, now military leader of Massachusetts Bay. They were greeted ceremonially by Bradford, Brewster, and Standish and gathered for a cordial meeting in Bradford's home. On Sunday morning,

---

[135] Edmund S. Morgan, *Visible Saints: The History of a Puritan Idea*, pp. 81-82.

* In his journal, Winthrop, not given to lavish praise, referred to Bradford as "a very discreet and grave man." (John Winthrop, *A History of New England 1630-1649*, James Kendall Hosmer, ed. [2 vols.; New York: Barnes and Noble, Inc., 1908], I, 93.) The rather warmer, more generous Bradford described Winthrop as "my much honored and beloved friend." (Bradford, *Of Plymouth Plantation*, p. 249.)

they attended services presided over by the pastor, Ralph Smith, and also involving Roger Williams which must have taxed the Christian charity of Winthrop in spite of his personal regard for the man. Bradford and a couple of other laymen also spoke. Later in the service, Winthrop and Wilson were invited to speak.[136] Although the practice of lay participation in services was characteristic of Plymouth, not Massachusetts Bay, Winthrop was drawn to the Pilgrims. At least for now, relations were cordial.

The Puritans were influenced toward congregationalism by their neighbors to the south. Without formally breaking with the Church of England, they were, in effect, congregationalist. Although overlooking Plymouth's separation, the English Church did seek to control larger, richer Massachusetts Bay, but never did succeed fully with these difficult people who professed allegiance to the Church, but in practice went their own way. Soon the home government was distracted by the difficulties between Charles I and Parliament, difficulties culminating in civil war, the execution of Charles, and the temporary overthrow of the monarchy.* Within a few years, Massachusetts Bay was as

---

[136] Bradford Smith, *Bradford of Plymouth*, pp. 252-253.

* In general, Plymouth sentiment, indeed that of New England as a whole, favored the Parliamentary forces (Roundheads) over the royalist Cavaliers. Yet neutrality prevailed, partially because the small colonies wanted to spare themselves involvement in the bitter, far-off war, but also because the two factions who comprised the Roundheads presented problems. The Presbyterians were unacceptable to the Congregationalist Pilgrims on the ground of church organization and the Independents, although in agreement with the Pilgrims on church organization, likewise were unacceptable because they espoused religious toleration, a position necessitated by the multitude of sects among them.

separatist/congregationalist as was Plymouth. Still, though, problems would continue.

In the spring of 1635, a trader named Hocking determined to establish a trading post on the Kennebec north of the Pilgrims' location in order to deal first with Indians coming south on the river with furs to trade. The Plymouth representatives, John Howland, the resident agent, and John Alden, who was there at the time, argued to no avail that their colony had jurisdiction over this area. Since he would not listen to reason, they then decided to take direct action by sending two men in a canoe to cut the cable on his ship. Spotting their approach, Hocking shot and killed one of the men whereupon the other slew Hocking. When Alden stopped at Boston on his way south, he was arrested by order of Governor Winthrop who was concerned that, even though his jurisdiction was questionable to say the least, unpunished crimes might be used by the English government as a justification for sending over a governor for all New England who would end the Puritan vision of a Christian society.

Plymouth, understandably furious at this usurpation of jurisdiction by Massachusetts Bay, sent Myles Standish to Boston to demand Alden's being freed from custody. Sending the fiery Standish testified to Plymouth's seriousness of purpose. The demand was refused, but Winthrop suggested that the case be adjudicated by a court with judges from both colonies. Plymouth accepted. The court placed the blame on Hocking. Since he had been employed by highly placed English interests, Plymouth sent Edward Winslow, their premier diplomat, to explain the incident and to head off further repercussions. When Thomas Morton*, the Pilgrims' old enemy, learned of Winslow's arrival, he stirred up

---

* See pp. 86-87.

William Laud, Archbishop of Canterbury, who was determined to uphold an Anglican high church position which included putting down Separatist and Puritan positions. Winslow, a layman, had taught in the Plymouth Church and, as a magistrate, had married people. This was enough for Laud to clap him in prison where he was held for several weeks until growing difficulties in England precursing the civil war which soon would ravage the realm, diverted Laud and led to Winslow's release.[137]

Relations between the colonies often would be strained as Massachusetts Bay grew rapidly into a powerful, expansionist neighbor, but Plymouth maintained its status during the lives of these remarkable men.

---

[137] Bradford, *Of Plymouth Plantation*, pp. 262-268; Dillon, *The Pilgrims*, pp. 213-214.

THE FRENCH

What today is Maine was a zone of conflict between the English and the French through the seventeenth century. As English colonies grew in New England, their circles of interest and influence spread westward and northward. Northward expansion brought them into conflict with the French moving south from the St. Lawrence River and from what today is Nova Scotia and New Brunswick. The English incursions into the Kennebec and Penobscot River areas increasingly incensed and alarmed the French since this region not only provided lucrative fur revenue, but also opened a back-door avenue of approach to Quebec, the heart of French Canada. Moving north on the Kennebec, an attacking enemy had but a few miles of land to cross before reaching the Chaudiere which could be followed to the St. Lawrence and Quebec. This was dramatically demonstrated by Benedict Arnold in 1775 when he led a force of Americans northward along this route and almost seized Quebec which by then was under English control.

In 1632, a French ship put into the Plymouth trading post on the Penobscot. At the time, the resident agent, Thomas Willet, was back in Plymouth procuring supplies. The French claimed that their ship was leaking and that they needed to haul her ashore for repairs. The men at the post were not sufficiently alert. The French, feigning friendliness as they looked over the store, suddenly turned on them and robbed the post of trade goods and pelts.[138]

Then in 1633, the Plymouth trading post at Mackias north of the Penobscot location was attacked. Two of the five men

---

[138]Bradford, *Of Plymouth Plantation*, pp. 245-246.

stationed there were killed, the other three captured, and all the trade goods there carried off.[139]

These were serious enough, but worse was to come two years later. In August 1635, the same month as the devastating hurricane*, the French attacked in greater strength, seized the Penobscot post and sent Willet and his men back to Plymouth with only their shallop and provisions for the trip. Stung by this aggression, Plymouth determined to recapture the post. Myles Standish and twenty militiamen were sent in the Plymouth bark.** In addition, the Great Hope, a well-armed ship commanded by a Captain Girling, was engaged for the project. If the attack were successful, he would receive 700 pounds of beaver pelts; if it were not, he would receive nothing. The potential payment was aboard the Plymouth bark.

The expedition arrived safely and, according to Bradford, could have retaken the post had they struck quickly. Girling, though, perhaps from cowardice, perhaps from sheer incompetence, opened fire from long range and soon ran out of powder since he had not brought much on his ship. The French suffered no casualties. Standish and the Plymouth contingent were not strong enough to recapture the post on their own.

Standish then learned that Girling intended to seize the Plymouth bark and take the beaver payment without fulfilling his end of the bargain. Standish successfully slipped

---

[139] Parkman, *France and England in North America*, Vol. I, p. 1079.

* See p. 63.

** A bark is a three-masted ship, square-rigged except for the aftermost one which is fore-and-aft-rigged.

out with his ship and returned home with it and the pelts. Apparently he did not have enough men to overcome Girling and his crew. Certainly the feisty Standish normally enjoyed a good scrap. Here he must have been substantially outnumbered and felt responsibility for the Plymouth ship and pelts. Otherwise it is not conceivable that he would take treachery such as that of Girling.

At this point, the government of Plymouth realized that the French now would reinforce and further fortify the position and that assistance from Massachusetts Bay would be needed for another expedition. Standish and Thomas Prence were sent to appeal for help based on the argument that a strong French presence would be a menace to all English settlements and interests. They received a response sympathetic in word, but no commitment to a joint operation. Massachusetts Bay was prepared to wish Plymouth well, but would not give any military assistance. Indeed, it soon came out that traders from Massachusetts Bay were doing business with the French at the Penobscot location. Long-term, Massachusetts Bay was more interested in acquiring Maine for itself than in helping Plymouth regain control.

Sadly, Plymouth did not have the power to defend its commercial enterprises against French assault, particularly in light of the inconsistent, even duplicitous attitude of Massachusetts Bay. Bradford commented sharply that English traders even sold powder and shot to the French. He stated that "it is no marvel though they still grow and encroach more and more upon the English, and fill the Indians with guns and munitions."[140] He continued that the English colonists were not as well-fortified as were the French and that serious trouble lay ahead. His analysis was

---

[140] Bradford, *Of Plymouth Plantation*, p. 279.

correct, but France was distracted by events elsewhere and did not put major resources into Maine. Had they done so, Bradford's words of warning would loom larger in our history. As it is, his castigation of those who chose financial profit over principle, even to trading with those who threaten the security of their country, lives on to this day as a reminder of the danger of not seeing beyond narrow self-interest.

THE NEW ENGLAND CONFEDERATION

In 1643, Massachusetts Bay, Plymouth, Connecticut, and New Haven joined together to form the New England Confederation.* The Articles of Confederation drawn up by representatives of these colonies proclaimed that "We all came into these parts of America with one and the same end and aim, namely, to advance the Kingdom of our Lord Jesus Christ and to enjoy the liberties of the Gospel in purity with peace...."[141] These men firmly believed that such a spiritual raison d'être was essential not only for the individual colonies, but also for the Confederation.

In order to enjoy the liberties and peace mentioned above, the colonial governments supported the Confederation as a military alliance against the Indians in the wake of the bitterly contested Pequot War and as a counter to the threat of Dutch expansion from the Hudson River area and by the French from Canada. Military operations would be supported proportionately by each colony based on the number of men between sixteen and sixty.[142] For example, when a campaign against the Narragansetts was contemplated in 1645 (conflict was averted), a force of 300 men was to be raised, of whom Massachusetts would provide 190, Plymouth 40, Connecticut 40, and New Haven 30.[143]

---

* Although commonly called the New England Confederation, it officially was designated the United Colonies of New England.

[141] Quoted in Gary DeMar, *America's Christian History: The Untold Story* (Atlanta, Georgia: American Vision, Publishers, Inc., 1993), p. 38.

[142] Bradford, *Of Plymouth Plantation*, p. 432.

[143] *Ibid.*, p. 340.

For the operation of the organization, two commissioners were elected annually from each of the colonies. All these men had to be in church fellowship. Six votes were necessary for a decision to be made. If this number could not be secured, the matter would be referred to the general courts (legislatures) of the colonies. The commissioners convened annually on the first Thursday in September, the meetings rotating between Boston, Hartford, New Haven, and Plymouth with the proviso that two consecutive meetings be held in Boston during each cycle.[144]

The Confederation worked to draw the colonies closer together. One area of contention was the policy of Massachusetts Bay to levy duties on goods of Plymouth, Connecticut, and New Haven being exported or imported through Boston. Connecticut had a toll on the trade of Springfield in Massachusetts Bay coming down or going up the Connecticut River. In 1650, Massachusetts Bay agreed to cease its practice if Connecticut did the same, a definite improvement.[145] The colonies also cooperated in supporting missionary work among the Indians, joining together to form the Society for the Propagation of the Gospel in New England.[146] In addition, the Confederation enjoyed some success in foreign relations. The 1644 Treaty of Boston avoided conflict with France over Nova Scotia, at least for a time, and the 1650 Treaty of Hartford solved a boundary dispute with the Dutch.

---

[144] *Ibid.*, p. 434.

[145] Osgood, *The Chartered Colonies. Beginnings of Self-Government*, p. 419.

[146] *Ibid.*, p. 422.

Serious debate arose among the Confederation members over whether to get involved in the Anglo-Dutch war of 1652-1654. Six commissioners voted to do so, but Massachusetts Bay declined, forcing neutrality since it was far and away the strongest of the member colonies.[147] Oliver Cromwell, Lord Protector of England after the overthrow of Charles I, had sought a coalition with the Netherlands to between them dominate the world outside Europe. The Dutch declined what for them would be a junior partnership since they had siphoned off a lot of England's trade during the years of civil strife which had torn that country apart in the 1640s and they no longer feared conquest by France. Cromwell then struck at Dutch commercial power through the Navigation Act of 1651 which required all trade with the exception of that from Europe to be carried in English or colonial ships. As far as trade with Europe was concerned, goods could be carried to English ports by ships from the country of origin. This was such a serious threat to Dutch commerce that war ensued. Slightly less than two years later, the war ended on terms favorable to England.[148] Apparently trade with New Amsterdam continued as the war largely was ignored in the colonies.[149]

The Confederation reached its peak of significance with the victorious conclusion of King Philip's War (1675-1676). After this war, though, danger from the Indians was much less and New Netherland had been seized by the English in

---

[147] David Hawke, *The Colonial Experience* (Indianapolis, Indiana: The Bobbs Merrill Company, Inc., 1966), p. 174.

[148] J. F. C. Fuller, *A Military History of the Western World*, Vol. II: *From the Defeat of the Spanish Armada, 1588 to the Battle of Waterloo, 1815* (New York: Funk and Wagnalls Company, 1955), p. 115.

[149] Hawke, *The Colonial Experience*, p. 190.

1664, removing the Dutch as a problem. Furthermore, Massachusetts Bay, the most powerful member, resented the equal representation. As a result of these factors, the Confederation was dissolved in 1684. Still, though, the colonies did gain experience in working together, especially in conducting joint military operations.

TWILIGHT

Bradford ceased writing his history in 1650. Arthur Quinn believed that he had become discouraged by the colonists' drifting away from sound faith and practice, that there was too much worldliness manifesting itself in pride, envy, and sexual immorality. By the standards of today, Plymouth would be regarded as a society with exemplary values overall. Bradford, though, remembered the vision of the founders, the sense of dedication and community which carried them through crises and he felt with a pang the declining fervor of a new generation which had not had to struggle and sacrifice as much for their faith.[150]

George Willison too believed that Bradford had ceased his writing because of discouragement at constantly recording setbacks in area after area, spiritual and moral difficulties, economic problems such as the loss of valuable fur trading opportunities in Maine and along the Connecticut River, the general fading before the growth of Massachusetts Bay, and the movement of people out of Plymouth town into new towns and new churches.[151]

In reference to the last point, Bradford understood well enough and welcomed the expansion of the colony beyond the town of Plymouth. After all, there wasn't that much good land nearby and the port as a trading center was being left behind by Boston. He wanted the town and church there, though, to continue into succeeding generations as the core of the colony. He lamented the decline of this status.

> And thus was this poor church left, like an ancient
> mother grown old and forsaken of her children,

---

[150] Quinn, *A New World*, pp. 81-88.

[151] Willison, *Saints and Strangers*, p. 333.

though not in their affections yet in regard of their bodily presence and personal helpfulness; her ancient members being most of them worn away by death, and these of later times being left like children translated into other families, and she like a widow left only to trust in God.[152]

In his biography of Bradford, Perry Westbrook considered the matter, listened to those who believed Bradford despaired, and concluded that his faith was triumphant. God's will is God's will--sometimes beyond the ken of human reason, but always accepted because of confidence in His knowing what is best. This is not mere passivity because Christians have the responsibility, the opportunity to serve God actively, striving to do what is right in His sight. The believers pray, do their best, then accept the results as Divine Providence. This Bradford did.[153]

No one knows with certainty what his thoughts were during these last years. By the time he stopped writing his history, he was about sixty. Even though saddened by a decline in fervor on the part of younger colonists who had not gone through the struggle of the vision-driven hard-core original settlers, it may have been more age than discouragement that led to the end of the journal. His faith remained strong until the end. Cotton Mather recorded that the day before he died in 1657, Bradford told those gathered at his bedside that "the Good Spirit of God had given him a

---

[152] Bradford, *Of Plymouth Plantation*, p. 334.

[153] Westbrook, *William Bradford*, pp. 150-151.

pledge of his happiness in another world and the first-fruits of his eternal glory."[154]

Cotton Mather was the scion of one of the most distinguished Massachusetts Bay Puritan families. He was the son of Increase Mather and the grandson of Richard Mather and John Cotton and a distinguished clergyman/scholar in his own right, authoring among other tomes *Magnalia Christi Americana* (*Christ's Great American Works*), one of the most significant early American histories which was published in London in 1702.

Born just a few years after the death of William Bradford, Mather had the opportunity to converse with those who had known Bradford and he observed Plymouth during its last years before it was absorbed into Massachusetts Bay. During his years of leadership, Bradford had earned the respect of John Winthrop and other leaders of the neighboring colony. Mather wrote of Bradford's learning, stating that he was fluent in Dutch, could get by in French, had mastered Hebrew, Greek, and Latin and was accomplished in theology, history, and philosophy. The highest accolade, though, was Mather's statement "But the crown of all was his holy, prayerful, watchful, and fruitful walk with God, wherein he was very exemplary."[155] As governor, he demonstrated great wisdom, exhibiting what Mather referred to as "prudence, justice, and moderation."[156] Ever the Massachusetts Bay

---

[154] Cotton Mather, *Magnalia Christi Americana* (2 vols.; Hartford, Connecticut: Silas Andrus and Son, 1855), I, p. 114.

[155] *Ibid.*

[156] *Ibid.*, pp. 111, 113.

Puritan, in a rather backhanded manner, he complimented Bradford for being free of Separatist extremism.[157]

In the compilation of Puritan writings which he edited with Thomas Johnson, Perry Miller too had high praise for Bradford, stating of him that:

No other writer will lead us so directly to the core of Puritanism as Bradford, none with such charm, generosity, largeness of spirit, with such calm assurance and massive strength will so completely reveal the essential frame of mind, the type of character, the quality of life that underlay the theology.[158]

A. L. Rowse, the eminent English historian of the Elizabethan era, also praised highly Bradford's work, stating that:

It has indeed the qualities that give enduring life to a book: absolute fidelity, lifelikeness and trustworthiness; its moral purity shines through, the selflessness, submission and control.[159]

William Bradford had made his mark as the first statesman in recorded American history. He was a man of Christian faith, rectitude, and ability who earned respect both within Plymouth and beyond its borders. He had vision, courage, and common sense. Furthermore, he was the first

---

[157] *Ibid.*, p. 113.

[158] Perry Miller and Thomas H. Johnson, eds., *The Puritans*, Vol. 1 (New York: Harper and Row, Publishers, 1963), p. 89.

[159] A. L. Rowse, *The Elizabethans and America* (New York: Harper and Brothers, 1959), p. 137.

American historian of note and one of the masters of English prose. Bradford left behind a legacy of examples in government and scholarship, but above all in Christian character.

FINALE

As the seventeenth century moved on, Massachusetts Bay grew substantially to become the most powerful colony north of Virginia. Economically, culturally, and numerically Plymouth declined in significance relative to its northern neighbor. As was stated earlier* the Puritans in England had more people and more financial resources than did the Separatists. Boston quickly became the major port of New England. Trade and fishing flourished. The fact that Plymouth had not received a royal charter and did not have powerful friends in England further weakened its prospects for continued separate status. Finally, a new generation was less fervent about the distinctives of Plymouth and more receptive to being part of a more powerful, more thriving colony.

In the autumn of 1691, Massachusetts Bay was granted a new charter which included Plymouth within its borders. Early in July of the next year, the General Court of Plymouth met for the last time and designated the last Wednesday of August "to be kept as a day of sollemne fasting and humiliation"[160] Within a few months, though, the people of Plymouth were reconciled and thanked God that Plymouth still was in the hands of the righteous.[161]

Plymouth never had the numbers, wealth, or university educated leadership of Massachusetts Bay, but in some respects their record is more extraordinary, more exemplary. They had less material prosperity, did not establish a

---

* See p. 88.

[160] Willison, *Saints and Strangers*, pp. 407-408.

[161] *Ibid.*, p. 408.

Harvard, achieved less in scholarship, but they were successful in much. Bradford Smith considered Plymouth "one of the most interesting experiments in government the world has ever seen."[162] They founded a Christian commonwealth which did not require church membership in order to vote although, as a practical matter, the leadership was separatist congregationalist. They set the precedent for a national day of Thanksgiving to God. They fostered market economics within a Christian context. On the whole, their dealings with the Indians, especially during Bradford's lifetime, were just and fair. They valued freedom, even extending a limited degree of toleration to those who differed from them, but freedom under God.

During the governorship of William Bradford, the moral environment of the colony was quite impressive. Pory said of Plymouth: "Now as concerning the quality of the people, how happy were it for our people in the Southern Colony [Virginia], if they were as free from wickedness and vice as these are in this place."[163] Also, de Rasieres commented on the strict laws there against fornication and adultery which were enforced on the Indians under the jurisdiction of the Pilgrims.[164]

The Pilgrims understood the Christian balance between the polar opposites of radical collectivism and radical individualism, forces which still threaten order, justice, and freedom today. Radical collectivism, if victorious, would grind the dignity, worth, and uniqueness of the individual beneath the impersonal wheels of an inexorably advancing,

---

[162] Smith, *Bradford of Plymouth*, p. 216.

[163] James, ed., *Three Visitors to Early Plymouth*, p. 11.

[164] Jameson, ed., *Narratives of New Netherland 1609-1664*, p. 112.

all powerful central government. Other institutions such as the church, the family, and local government will fall before the onslaught of this behemoth. Radical individualism bows down before the autonomous individual, rejecting the authority of the traditional, cohesive elements of civilization, turning away from revelation and tradition, producing an atomized society of rootless persons.

Society is an organic whole. This is especially true of Christian society such as the Pilgrims labored to establish in Plymouth. This does not mean that the individual is unimportant. Although there are wide variations in calling, intelligence, ability and dedication among people, all have rights, responsibilities, and opportunities. The individual, however, is a part of a whole--the church, the nation--and is truly fulfilled through it. Where the sense of community prevails, individuals acknowledge themselves to be part of something which is greater than themselves.

In Western Civilization, the church is the outstanding example of community. It is presented in Scripture as the body of Christ of which all Christians are members. In Romans 12:4-6, the teaching is presented that:

For just as we have many members in one body and all the members do not have the same function, so we, who are many, are one body in Christ, and individually members one of another. And since we have gifts that differ according to the grace given us....

The following is set forth in I Corinthians 12:12-14:

For even as the body is one and yet has many members and all the members of the body, though they are many, are one body, so also is Christ.

For by one Spirit we were all baptized into one body,
whether Jews or Greeks, whether slaves or free, and
we were all made to drink of one Spirit.

For the body is not one member, but many.

Just as the human body consists of divers organs forming
an organic entity, so Christian society, composed of
individuals with varying abilities, interests, and personalities,
constitutes an organic entity. The human hand is most
remarkable in its capability of performing many intricate
tasks. If, however, it is cut off, its significance has been lost.
It is still recognizable as a hand, but because it has been
severed from the body, it no longer has any real import.
Thus it is with the person who turns away from community.

So the Pilgrims believed. Many have called them
democratic in that the franchise was widely extended for the
time, church and government leaders were freely elected by
the freemen, and, in general, market economics prevailed. Yet
they were not democratic individualists. Individual will and
choice operated within the parameters of Biblical teachings.
Always the Pilgrims were Christians above all else.

They gave many enduring examples for future
generations. Devout Christian faith, integrity, hard work,
and courage were their hallmarks. To this time and to these
people we Americans, regardless of denominational
affiliation, may turn with confidence when seeking
inspiration and guidance in the application of Christian
beliefs to public policy. Admittedly, they were narrow in
some of their ways, such as education, especially that of girls,
yet most assuredly they laid a firm foundation upon which
the United States would grow and become the greatest

country in the world, an example for all of order, justice, and freedom.

BIBLIOGRAPHY

Primary Sources

Bradford, William. *Of Plymouth Plantation*, Samuel Eliot
Morison, ed. New York: Alfred W. Knopf, 1996.

James, Sidney V., ed. *Three Visitors to Early Plymouth*. Bedford,
Massachusetts: Applewood Books, 1997.

Jameson, J. Franklin, ed. *Narratives of New Netherland 1609-
1664*. New York: Charles Scribner's Sons, 1909.

Miller, John, ed. *The Colonial Image: Origins of American
Culture*. New York: George Braziller, 1962.

Miller, Perry and Johnson, Thomas, eds. *The Puritans*. 2 vols.
New York: Harper and Row, Publishers, 1963.

Morton, Nathaniel. *New England's Memoriall*. Bowie,
Maryland: Heritage Books, Inc., 1997.

Mourt, G. *Mourt's Relation*. Bedford, Massachusetts: Applewood
Books, 1963.

Williams, Roger. *Limits of the Civil Magistrate*, in Polishook, Irwin
H., ed., *Roger Williams, John Cotton and Religious Freedom*.
Englewood Cliffs, New Jersey: Prentice-Hall, Inc., 1967.

Winslow, Edward. *Winslow's Relation: Good Newes from New
England*. Bedford, Massachusetts: Applewood Books, n.d.

Winthrop, John. *A History of New England 1630-1649*, James Kendall Hosmer, ed., 2 vols. New York: Barnes and Noble, Inc., 1908.

Secondary Sources

Adams, James Truslow. *The March of Democracy: A History of the United States*, Vol. I: *The Rise of the Union*. New York: Charles Scribner's Sons, 1933.

Andrews, Charles. *The Colonial Period of American History*, Vol. I: *The Settlements*. New Haven, Connecticut: Yale University Press, 1964.

Bolton, Herbert Eugene and Marshall, Thomas Maitland. *The Colonization of North America 1492-1783*. New York: The Macmillan Company, 1920.

Boorstin, Daniel J. *Hidden History*. New York: Harper and Row, 1987.

Churchill, Winston S. *A History of the English Speaking Peoples*, Vol. II: *The New World*. New York: Dodd, Mead and Company, 1956.

Covey, Cyclone. *The Gentle Radical: A Biography of Roger Williams*. New York: The Macmillan Company, 1966.

DeMar, Gary. *America's Christian History: The Untold Story*. Atlanta, Georgia: American Vision, Publishers, Inc., 1993.

Demos, John. *A Little Commonwealth: Family Life in Plymouth Colony*. New York: Oxford University Press, 1970.

Dillon, Francis. *The Pilgrims*. Garden City, New York: Doubleday and Company, Inc., 1975.

Fleming, Thomas J. *One Small Candle: The Pilgrim's First Year in America*. New York: W. W. Norton and Company, Inc., 1964.

Fuller, J. F. C. *A Military History of the Western World*, Vol. II: *From the Defeat of the Spanish Armada, 1588 to the Battle of Waterloo, 1815*. New York: Funk and Wagnalls Company, 1955.

Hare, Lloyd C. M. *Thomas Mayhew, Patriarch to the Indians 1593-1682*. New York: AMS Press, 1964.

Hawke, David. *The Colonial Experience*. Indianapolis, Indiana: The Bobbs Merrill Company, Inc., 1966.

Horowitz, David. *The First Frontier: The Indian Wars and America's Origins: 1607-1776*. New York: Simon and Schuster, 1978.

Kirk, Russell. *America's British Culture*. New Brunswick, New Jersey: Transaction Publishers, 1993.

___. *The Roots of American Order*. La Salle, Illinois: Open Court, 1977.

Kittredge, Henry C. *Cape Cod: Its People and Their History*. Boston: Houghton Mifflin Company, 1968.

Langdon, Gorge D., Jr. *Pilgrim Colony: A History of New Plymouth 1621-1691*. New Haven, Connecticut: Yale University Press, 1966.

Leach, Douglas Edward. *Arms For Empire: A Military History of the British Colonies in North America, 1607-1763*. New York: The Macmillan Company, 1973.

Lippy, Charles H., Choquette, Robert, and Poole, Stafford. *Christianity Comes to the Americas*. New York: Paragon House, 1992.

Marshall, Peter and Manuel, David. *The Light and the Glory*. Old Tappan, New Jersey: Fleming H. Revell Company, 1977.

Mather, Cotton. *Magnalia Christi Americana*. Hartford, Connecticut: Silas Andrus and Son, 1855.

Middlekauff, Robert. *The Mathers: Three Generations of Puritan Intellectuals, 1596-1728*. New York: Oxford University Press, 1971.

Millard, Catherine. *The Rewriting of America's History*. Camp Hill, Pennsylvania: Horizon House Publishers, 1991.

Morgan, Edmund S. *Roger Williams: The Church and the State*. New York: Harcourt, Brace and World, Inc., 1967.

___. *Visible Saints: The History of a Puritan Idea*. New York: New York University Press, 1963.

Morison, Samuel Eliot. *By Land and By Sea*. New York: Alfred E. Knopf, 1953.

___. *The Intellectual Life of Colonial New England*. New York: New York University Press, 1965.

____. *The Oxford History of the American People*. New York: Oxford University Press, 1965.

Nock, Albert J. *Our Enemy, The State*. Tampa, Florida: Halberg Publishing Corporation, 1996.

North, Gary. *Puritan Economic Experiments*. Tyler, Texas: Institute for Christian Economics, 1988.

Osgood, Herbert L. *The American Colonies in the Seventeenth Century*, Vol. I: *Chartered Colonies. Beginnings of Self-Government*. Gloucester, Massachusetts: Peter Smith, 1957.

Parkman, Francis. *France and England in North America*. 2 vols. New York: Literary Classics of the United States, Inc., 1983.

Perry, Ralph Barton. *Puritanism and Democracy*. New York: The Vanguard Press, 1944.

Peterson, Robert. *In His Majesty's Service: Christians in Politics*. Lafayette, Louisiana: Huntington House Publishers, 1995.

Quinn, Arthur. *A New World: An Epic of Colonial America from the Founding of Jamestown to the Fall of Quebec*. New York: Berkeley Books, 1994.

Rouse, A. L. *The Elizabethans and America*. New York: Harper and Brothers, 1959.

Rutman, Darrett B. *Husbandmen of Plymouth: Farms and Villages in the Old Colony, 1620-1692*. Boston: Beacon Press, 1967.

Schneider, Paul. *The Enduring Shore: A History of Cape Cod, Martha's Vineyard, and Nantucket*. New York: Henry Holt and Company, 2000.

Singer, C. Gregg. *A Theological Interpretation of American History*. Nutley, New Jersey: The Craig Press, 1964.

Smith, Bradford. *Bradford of Plymouth*. Philadelphia: J. B. Lippincott Company, 1951.

Stratton, Eugene Aubrey. *Plymouth Colony: Its History and People 1620-1691*. Salt Lake City: Ancestry Publishing, 1986.

Waldman, Carl. *Atlas of the North American Indian*. New York: Facts on File Publications, 1985.

Westbrook, Perry D. *William Bradford*. Boston: Twayne Publishers, 1978.

Willison, George F. *Saints and Strangers*. New York: Reynal and Hitchcock, 1945.

_____. *The Pilgrim Reader: The Story of the Pilgrims As Told by Themselves and Their Contemporaries Friendly and Unfriendly*. Garden City, New York: Doubleday and Company, Inc., 1953.

Wood, Betty. *The Origins of American Slavery: Freedom and Bondage in the English Colonies*. New York: Hill and Wang, 1997.

INDEX

William vii viii ix 1 2 3 5n 6-9 12 14-16 19-24 26-28
31 32 35 37 40 41 43-51 53-58 63 65 67-70 72 75
77-80 82 83 86 88-90 94-96 101-103 105 107
William, Jr. 27
BRAINTREE 86
BREWSTER, Jonathan 26 76
William 1 2 8 12 20 25 26 30 59 76 89
BROWNE, John 46
BURKE, Edmund 55
BUTTEN, William 8
CALVIN, John 2
CAMBRIDGE UNIVERSITY 1 30 32 34 38 52 88
CAPE ANN 88
CAPE COD vii 8-10 15 17 53 59 63 65 70-72 89
CAPE COD CANAL 63
CARVER, John 8 11 22 23
CASTINE 63
CHARLES I 37 64 90 99
CHATHAM 70
CHAUNCY, Charles 32 33
CHURCH 1-3 8 11 29-31 33-41 45 47 50 52 55 70 82 83
88-90 92 98 101 107-109
CLARK, Thomas 64
CLASS SYSTEM 55
COKE, Edward 34
COLLIER, William 47
COMMUNALISM 41 56 57
CONANACUS 79
CONNECTICUT 28 33 59 63 75-77 81 97 98 101
CORBITANT 68 69 73 81
COTTON, John 32 40 99 102 103
CROMWELL, Oliver 99

LAUD, William 92

LEYDEN 3 5 6 8 27 30 58 88

LITTLE JAMES, the 31 61

LOCKE, John 11 12

LOTHROP, John 38

LUTHER, Martin 2

LYFORD, John 30 31 32

MACKIAS 93

MAINE 21 46 59 63 95 96 101

MANOMET INDIANS 85

MARCUS AURELIUS 2

MARTHA'S VINEYARD 72

MASHPEE 71

MASON, John 77

MASSACHUSETTS BAY viii 24 32-34 37-40 44-48 52
    53 62 65 70-72 75-77 87-92 95 97-101 103 106

MASSACHUSETTS INDIANS 18 24 85

MASSASOIT 21 24 25 67-69 72-74 79 85

MAYFLOWER COMPACT ix 9

MAYFLOWER, the 6-9 14 15 17 19 20 23 28 48

MAYFLOWER II, the vii

MAYHEW, Thomas ix 72
    Thomas, Jr. 72

MERCHANT TAYLORS 33

MERRY MOUNT 87

MIDDLEBOROUGH 68

MILITIA 27 45 67 80 83 85

MILLER, Perry 109

MIXED MULTITUDE 8 49

MOHAWK INDIANS 78

MOHEGAN INDIANS 75 77

MORISON, Samuel Eliot viii ix 7 13

John M. Pafford, a protégé of Russell Kirk, is an ordained clergyman and has been a professor of history and philosophy at Northwood University in Midland, Michigan since 1976. In 1995, Dr. Pafford received the Northwood University Award for Faculty Excellence. Earlier, he taught at Highland College, Pasadena, California; the University of Baltimore, Baltimore, Maryland; Fairfax Christian School, Fairfax, Virginia; and Perkiomen School, Pennsburg, Pennsylvania.

Dr. Pafford has served as chairman of the Michigan Republican Issues Committee, chairman of the Michigan Conservative Union, co-chairman of Michigan Scholars for Reagan-Bush, Michigan vice chairman of the Forbes presidential campaign, and is a member of the Board of Scholars of the Mackinac Center for Public Policy. Back in the 1960s, he was chairman of Young Americans for Freedom in two states.

He is an experienced radio and television commentator and is the author of numerous articles on history, theology, and contemporary events.

He and his wife, Martha, are the parents of four and have eight grandchildren.

For recreation, Dr. Pafford enjoys tennis, reading, opera, and nature, especially the ocean and the Great Lakes.